ALLIED
DUNBAR

Are You Managing Facilities?

Getting the Best Out of Buildings

John Grigg   Alan Jordan

NICHOLAS BREALEY
PUBLISHING
LONDON

First published by
Nicholas Brealey Publishing Limited in 1993
156 Cloudesley Road
London N1 0EA

in association with
The Industrial Society
48 Bryanston Square
London W1H 7LN
Telephone: 071 262 2401

ISBN 1 85788 0242

© Allied Dunbar Financial Services Limited 1993

Illustrations by David James

British Library Cataloguing in Publication Data
A catalogue record for this book is available from the
British Library.

Allied Dunbar Assurance plc
Allied Dunbar Centre
Swindon SN1 1EL
Tel: 0793 514514

Typeset by The Setting Studio, Newcastle upon Tyne
Printed and bound in Finland by
Werner Söderstrom Oy

ALLIED DUNBAR

Other Books in the Series

ARE YOU MANAGING?
A Guide to Good Management
Peter Stemp

ARE YOU MANAGING YOUR HEALTH?
A Guide to a Balanced Lifestyle
Dr H. Beric Wright

ARE YOU MANAGING PURCHASING?
A Guide to Better Buying
Malcolm Jones

CONTENTS ─────────────────

Foreword John Crawshaw

1 Introduction   **1**

What is facilities management?   1
What are the main functions?   3
Who is responsible for FM?   4
How to use this book   4

2 Property Strategy   **7**

The importance of property strategy   8
Strategic space planning   9
Specification of long term space   13
Evaluation criteria   14
Refurbishment options   17
A simple case study   17
Some practical points   18
Checklist   21

3 Managing Space   **23**

The significance of premises costs   23
Formulating a successful strategy   24
Evaluate the existing situation   25
Understand the business plan   28
Focus on real costs   28
Agree targets   29
Flexible solutions   29
Setting your guidelines   30
Open plan factors   30
Fixed space   31

Standard layouts   32
Contingency   33
Department locations   34
Benefits   34
Some common issues   35
Office moves   37
Computer aided design   41
Total quality environment   42
Checklist   43

4   Cost Control   45

The cost control cycle   45
Budgeting   46
Life cycle costing   49
Forecasting   50
Cost control actions   51
Expenditure tracking   53
Capital works   54
Time   54
Quality   55
Costs   56
Checklists   57

5   The Management of Outsourcing   61

Typical contracted services   62
Organisation of contracted services   63
Purchasing skills   67
Working with contractors   68
Contractor selection   69
Specification setting   70
Initial contact   73
Contractor vetting   74
Short listing   76
Contractor performance   76
Single source contractors   79
Checklist   82

6   Negotiating and Achieving a Good Contract   85

Competition   86

CONTENTS

	What to negotiate?	87
	Do's and Don'ts in negotiation	89
	Achieving a good contract	91
	Model contracts	92
	Checklist	94

7 Maintenance   **97**

	Maintenance control	97
	Centrally located premises	98
	Standards	99
	Maintenance classifications	99
	Reactive maintenance	100
	Planned maintenance	100
	Cyclic maintenance	101
	Cyclic maintenance checks	101
	Attic stock	102
	Maintenance manuals	103
	Maintenance contracts	104
	Schedule of rates/day work	105
	Materials selection	106
	Multiple locations	107
	Central control	108
	Organisation	108
	Guidelines	109
	Contractors' register	110
	Authorisation	111
	Invoices	111
	Engineering maintenance	112
	Checklist	121

8 Energy Management   **125**

	Monitoring and targeting: measuring efficiency	126
	The concept of energy centres and drivers	127
	Degree days	128
	Air-conditioning	130
	Establishing monitoring & targeting	131
	Source choices and tariffs	133
	Opportunities and vulnerabilities	137
	CHP and private generation	137

Interruptible fuel arrangements   138
Competence of site personnel   139
Contract energy management   139
Energy-saving initiatives   140
Typical methods for saving energy in offices   143
Estimating payback   145
Checklist   146

9   Office Services   149

Raising the profile   149
Strategic thinking   150
Contingency plans   151
Sharing the vision   152
Operational issues   153
Checklist   156

10   Health and Safety   159

Facilities' manager's role within   160
health and safety
Specific areas of interest   161
Main legislative framework   162
Health and safety procedures for contractors   164
Principal legislation   165
The working environment   176
Checklist   181

11   Business Relocation   185

Reasons for business relocations   185
Project management of a move   186
'D-Day' – the actual move   189
Relocation do's and don'ts   196
An opportunity for a change   196
Checklist   202

**12   Green Issues and the Working   205
       Environment**

Facilities and the environment   205
Setting up   207

CONTENTS

Building fabric and services 210
Company cars/transport 213
Waste management and recycling 215
Communication and involvement 217
Checklist 219

13 Facilities Management for Small Business 221

The relevance of FM 222
Cost grouping 222
Apportioning responsibility 223
A management approach 223
Annual audits 224
Checklist 225

14 TQM for Facilities Management 227

TQM history and definition 228
How does TQM apply to
facilities management? 229
Principles of TQM 230
Implementing TQM 235
Communication 238
Supplier/contractor involvement 239
Checklist 240

15 Property and Legal Issues 243

Some key property-related terms 243
Property ownership 244
Leasing 245
Statutory controls 245
The uniform business rate 246
Service charges 248
VAT 250
JCT contracts 251
Building regulations 252
Checklist 252

About the Authors 254
Acknowledgement 255

FOREWORD

Since the late 1970's, facilities management has developed faster than almost any other professional discipline. Its rapid rise has outpaced criticism that it is simply a marketing platform, or an attempt to exaggerate the importance of a group of specialist middle managers. For the real significance of the function lies not just in the effective resourcing of support services, but in the professional management of all physical resources which underpin the ability of organisations to do business - and above all to develop and change with time and circumstances. Its growth owes as much to the increasing complexity of technology in modern buildings, and the need to satisfy a more knowledgeable and demanding body of users, as it does to the desire to reduce operating costs.

Recognition of these issues is rapidly transforming the way facilities are managed in the public and private sectors – from offices through to healthcare, leisure and educational buildings. And the facilities management movement is gathering pace in a truly international sense: from its north American origins, it has now spread to the UK, Europe, Australasia, the Far East and Japan.

But the comparative newness of the profession still makes definitions difficult. More than five years ago it was claimed that no two facilities managers shared exactly the same set of responsibilities, nor were they likely to hold identical positions within the management hierarchy – and this still applies to some extent today.

Job responsibilities are wide – ranging and numerous, and involve coordinating multiple disciplines such as:

- Estate/property acquisition and/or disposal.
- Procurement and management of services such as cleaning, catering, laundry and security, and other general administration.
- Space planning and design, including the building engineering and information technology infrastructure.
- Architecture and construction.
- Maintenance and operations management.
- Ergonomics and health and safety.

Individual responsibilities vary tremendously: some managers, for example, may handle estate and property issues in addition to space planning and design, engineering and support services. Others may have a greater focus on administration, health and safety or technology. To make matters worse, comparatively few are known as 'facilities managers' – although this is beginning to change.

However difficult the generalisations remain, a common thread binds facilities managers together and reinforces their contribution to overall business performance. For as coordinators of such a wide range of technical skills, facilities managers are in a unique position to set and maintain quality standards in the working environment, and to help improve briefing and decision-making by providing data on how their buildings are performing. They also have an increasing important role to play in terms of accountability for safety standards and for ensuring that staff are protected from potential health hazards, such as Legionnaires' Disease.

The educational task involved in communicating these messages effectively to organisations and practitioners is considerable. It was a major factor in the creation in 1986 of the UK's professional body, The Association of Facilities Managers, and is the reason why, as a group, we remain committed to encouraging publications such as 'Are You Managing Facilities?'

Both share a common purpose, which is to promote the highest standards of professional practice and to demonstrate, in a very practical sense, the benefits of applying effective facilities management to organisations in all sectors. The book combines discussions of principles with checklists, references and, perhaps most important of all, advice which stems from direct experience of facilities management gathered over many years.

If, as one commentator has suggested, facilities management remains, 'at the leading edge of some of the greatest questions of our time', those involved will face increasing challenges – particularly in reconciling the diverse demands of space, technology and people. There may even come a time when facilities managers will be more concerned to balance the interest of workers in hundreds or thousands of small, widely dispersed sites than to focus on larger work centres. But whatever lies ahead for the development of organisations, facilities management will continue to plot a positive parallel course – and publications of this kind can only help lay a solid foundation on which the profession can build.

John Crawshaw
Director
The Association of Facilities Managers

CHAPTER ONE

INTRODUCTION

This book is not written for experts in facilities management. Each chapter could form the basis of a sizeable tome if this were the intention. It aims instead to be an easy reference for busy managers from different backgrounds – an easy-to-read format and checklist outlining the principles of successful facilities management. These principles have been developed within First Move Facilities Management – FM^2 – during a 20 year period working with clients and supporting the nationwide growth of a large parent company.

What is facilities management?

The term facilities management, or FM, has been coined in recent years to describe the management of buildings, infrastructure and support services. Formal definitions are many, various and sometimes confusing. Colleagues from similar sectors often express individual interpretations – for example, 'Computer FM', which deals specifically with different aspects of computer services management.

Another view is that facilities management is the name given to the process of employing external contractors to provide support services, although the expressions 'outsourcing' or 'contracting out' are gaining recognition as more meaningful alternatives to this particular aspect of FM. However, outsourcing is not an alternative definition for FM; it is only part of the sphere of activities within facilities management. Out of this background of misunderstanding a common view of facilities management has taken shape among property and support services specialists – it is the coordination of buildings, work and people into a single interactive system.

In this book, FM deals with electricity consumption and environmental issues, company culture and contract maintenance; security and space allocation; costs and catering. In other words, a diverse range of vital activities which can be simply summed up as 'getting the best from buildings'.

Following a growing realisation that working environments are important in terms of productivity and operating costs as well as recruitment and staff retention, concern for these issues has moved from the boiler room to the boardroom. Moreover, property and facilities often represent more than 30% of a company's assets, and many organisations have recognised that premises costs are frequently second only to staff costs in the corporate budget. It is not surprising therefore that facilities management has started to emerge as a distinct profession.

As this critical role that facilities departments can play has increased in profile, there has been a corresponding demand for more information on the profession. Every year new research and innovations are introduced and a number of associations have been founded over the past 10 years to further the development of facilities management. A number of associations or FM organisations have been formed over the last decade throughout Europe and the rest of the world. In addition FM has found its way into degree courses and universities are beginning to offer higher degrees with FM as the core subject.

What are the main functions?

Quite simply, facilities management can be all things to all men. The term has been used to define all kinds of support services outside the main core business. Traditionally it can include:

- Lease terms and negotiations
- Rent reviews
- Building services
- Engineering maintenance
- Project management
- Space management
- Cleaning and security
- Catering
- Office services
- Budgets and cost control
- IT, voice and data
- Purchasing and contract negotiation
- Car fleet management
- Graphic services and reprographics.

Facilities management therefore embraces a series of vital functions to support all types of organisations using any and every type of building. This is true of factories, warehouses, hotels, offices, laboratories, hospitals, computer centres, theatres, schools and airports – in fact every conceivable shape and size of accommodation used for any conceivable purpose.

The same rationale holds firm regardless of geographical location; whether your organisation operates worldwide or is confined to a small town; and whether your business uses an elaborate network of nationwide branches or operates from a "back office" central HQ complex. It is relevant to large or small organisations, and in recognising this we have included a chapter on FM for smaller businesses which gives guidelines on how to approach the control of support costs.

Who is responsible for FM?

The organisational structure of a facilities management department can be equal in diversity to the types of property to be serviced. A major factor is the size of the operation and the geographical spread of the portfolio. Thus, in a relatively small company perhaps the Personnel Manager or Finance Director will carry responsibility for all property management issues.

An organisation which occupies nationwide offices will probably include a large facilities department to manage a significant budget. In some cases this function may be located in a central HQ, or may extend to a regionally based network of facilities managers with specific knowledge of local regional conditions and contacts. Similarly, a large department may include various professionally qualified experts in such fields as general estate management, building surveying, quantity surveying, building services engineering, architecture and interior design. Some might even count lawyers and accountants amongst their numbers.

How to use this book

Facilities management involves a wide spectrum of activities and, in all its various guises, will fulfil a vital role in most business organisations. The contents of this book will no doubt reinforce much of what you already do but may also provide a few reminders on other aspects (perfect facilities managers are few and far between!)

The book deliberately starts with issues relating to property and managing space as these are the main 'drivers' for most FM issues. The type and use of space will often dictate what type of support services are subsequently employed and the cost of those services. It is in the support area, which includes services such as cleaning, security, reprographics and so on where the topical outsourcing debate is being carried out.

Please use it as a refresher or for reference depending on your experience and needs. You can read it from cover to cover or refer to specific topics – or both! If you follow the advice you should find that you are managing your facilities better.

CHAPTER TWO

PROPERTY STRATEGY

For any organisation to operate successfully it needs people, equipment and material – and property in which to house the people, equipment and material. Building size and design, workforce availability, customer base, communications and occupational costs (measured against affordability) will often be the major criteria for selecting the preferred location for your organisation. The plans for meeting these various requirements are normally referred to as 'property strategy', and your aim is to ensure that the right property is available at the right time and place, and at the right cost.

This chapter explains the steps necessary to develop your property strategy:

- Strategic space planning
- Specification of requirements
- Evaluation criteria

It also provides some practical advice on refurbishment and gives a simple case study.

The importance of property strategy

In most cases, property represents the second biggest outlay after payroll and so the costly burden of too much space needs to be avoided. Perhaps worse still is having too little space, which could severely inhibit your operations and thus prove to be financially disastrous. This principle holds equally true for a large multi-national or for a small professional office.

A complete property strategy has three distinct items:

- It is the procedure which if followed will ensure that you meet the organisation's requirement for space as closely as possible, ie minimising surplus but never running out. Acquiring and, depending on the market, disposing of space can be a lengthy process – designing and building an office block can take three years for example. However, most businesses need to react quickly to their changing markets, and it requires careful planning and a sound approach to be able to react to these changing requirements with minimal disruption.
- It should specify the facilities and standards the company needs with its property. Even within office blocks, design standards for floor width, cabling systems and air conditioning can vary dramatically. Indeed, in certain circumstances air-conditioning may be considered unnecessary. The specification of facilities and standards should define the ideal space for the particular organisation and the definition should be kept up to date.
- Finally, a property strategy should define the criteria to be used for decision making. Most of these criteria will be financial, eg which costs to include and how to compare alternatives. They should cover both acquisition/disposal decisions, and actions required to maintain the value of the property.

Let's look at these three areas in more detail.

Strategic space planning

There are two sides to the strategic space planning exercise – supply and demand. The objective is to make these balance as closely as possible (with supply always exceeding demand). The steps that should be followed to achieve this are shown in Figure 2.1 and may be described as follows:

- The long term trend in staff numbers (growth or reduction) should be identified by looking at historical data, taking into account overall corporate strategy (property strategy must be an integral part of corporate planning). Clearly this growth trend will not be maintained every year. However, as property strategy is essentially long term, it is the average growth rate over a number of years that is used in planning the space requirement (15 Note 2 at Figure 2.1).
- The 'square feet per person' is the other key factor in determining the demand for space. Two points are important here:
  - Property costs are dictated essentially by the number of square feet in the portfolio. Reducing the average square feet per person (Note 3 at Figure 2.1) from 130 to 115 will reduce property costs by approximately 10% – a very significant number! But remember – in some cases you have to dispose of the surplus to realise these savings.
  - A suitable unit of measurement for the area must be used. Gross floor area or net floor area (the units normally used in property matters) are not ideal for space planning. It's better to use a figure such as usable floor area which relates to the practical use of the space – ignoring areas such as lobbies, restaurants, and primary circulation space. These should be allowed for separately in your calculations.
- The space required to accommodate people can be calculated by multiplying the number of staff at a

SUMMARY OF SPACE REQUIRED OVER 5 YEARS

Year	1993	1994	1995	1996	1997
Estimated Growth	4%	6%	6%	6%	6%
Staff	1,000	1,040	1,102	1,168	1,238
Occupational Space (Kft^2)	130	135.2	143.3	151.8	160.9
Fixed Element Space (Kft^2)	10.4	11	11	11	12
Space Required (Kft^2)	140.4	146.2	154.3	162.8	172.9
Space Available (Kft^2)	158	158	158	114*	80*
Surplus (Kft^2) /(Shortfall)	17.6	11.2	3.3	(48.8)	(92.9)

* - Lease expires

Notes:
1. All figures are based on usable space.
2. Estimated growth as per business projections.
3. Occupational space based on average usable space per head of 130 sq ft.
4. Staff excluded in fixed elements.
5. Space required = Occupational Space + Fixed Space
6. Space available measured in net usable sq ft.
7. Projected imbalance used for planning acquisitions (or disposals).

(Figure 2.1)

particular point in time by the average square feet per person. Staff who do not require an average space allocation – eg security, switchboard, computer operators – should be dealt with separately (Note 4 at Figure 2.1). The space required for these functions should be added in to give a total space. Hence, the formula is:

Total usable space required = (number of staff occupying space x space per person) + space for specific functions (Note 5 at Figure 2.1).

- Using this approach coupled with the long term growth rate or decline in the number of staff will give you a matrix showing the demand for space in usable square feet over a period of time (Note 5 at Figure 2.1).
- The supply of space is devised by evaluating the existing building stock in the same usable terms i.e. the area required to operate the building such as plant rooms and lobbies should be ignored leaving only the number of square feet that can be used for staff. This space available should be plotted over time taking into account end of leases or additional space becoming available to produce a supply matrix (Note 6 at Figure 2.1).
- Comparing the supply and demand matrices (now both in the same terms) will show where there is likely to be a shortfall (or an excess of space) if the long term trend holds true. It is this mismatch that is the basis of the property strategy process. A programme of acquisition (or disposal) must be established to meet this imbalance (Note 7 at Figure 2.1).

Developing a building to meet an organisation's specific requirement can take three years, so the plan must be 3-5 years in duration. Within this time frame there will clearly be many options to consider and this is dealt with later. However, in essence, the property strategy is a plan which cost effectively matches the demand and supply for space, measured in the same units, over the long term.

When a solution to any mismatch is agreed, it should be included in the supply matrix. This will then contain the available square feet if the actions identified are carried through.

- Of course, the one thing that is true of any average such as a growth trend, is that at any point of time it will not be accurate! If the real rate of staff growth varies from the planning average then short term contingency actions must be taken to meet this change. This will either be acquiring rented space on a short term lease, or on a lease with a break clause, or sub letting space on a short term let. In essence, short term variations from the long term trend should be accommodated by short term actions. Again, these acquisitions or disposals should be built into the supply matrix.

- This approach inevitably leads to a mixture of long term 'core' space, acquired to meet the long term trend, and short term contingency space. This mixed portfolio offers the opportunity to match supply and demand closely by careful management. For example, if a larger long term building is planned for three years in the future, it may be possible to acquire short term space with a lease which terminates when the new space becomes available. This will smooth out the growth in supply and allow excess space to be minimised.

- Although the amount of space to acquire will be determined by the long term demand trend and how this interacts with the supply, it is advisable to have some contingency space to contain changing demands for, say, one year ahead.

A similar process can be tailored for all types of businesses and organisations, large or small. Whether your company comprises 3,000 staff or only 30, property and services costs will always represent a significant proportion of your outgoings.

Specification of long term space

The specification should be on two levels. It should define, in overall terms, the type of space which matches ideally the company's requirements. Secondly, it should specify in detail the standards that should be met and facilities that should be provided.

Dealing with these in turn, the key high level factors are as follows:

Location

This can cover different aspects ranging from which country would be acceptable to which part of the town in which a company should be located. (With most retailers, location is the top priority, some requirements are within 50 yards of a particular position in the High Street!)

When choosing a location or considering a relocation, a company needs to tie this in with its business objectives. The questions which need to be considered include:

- Is it necessary to be close to its market or suppliers, or even its competitors?
- What are the relative property costs in each location?
- Is there a good supply of well trained staff?
- What facilities are needed to attract staff, eg car parking, public transport, town centre shopping?
- What are the relative salaries in each area?
- Is there plenty of space for future expansion?

These points illustrate the importance of making the right decisions on location and the importance of clearly establishing the criteria.

Building type

Once you have established where you want to be located, you are then faced with acquiring your space. Here again you need to refer back to what the business requirements are. A large admin-based company with virtually a VDU per person may not be able to function effectively in a poorly air- conditioned 1970's building with small floors. Does the organisation require its own front door, or perhaps a high percentage of fixed offices? These are the types of questions which you will need to ask.

An experienced facilities manager will know only too well the problems of trying to make the wrong type of building work for the organisation. It is worth spending time up front in setting out these criteria.

The space must satisfy these requirements fully both now and in the foreseeable future. Any compromise will ultimately be expensive. On the other hand, space acquired to meet short term variations will probably not fit the ideal definition. The greater the difference, the more it will reduce the flexibility to move people and equipment within the total portfolio.

The detailed document – the specification of standards and facilities – is required when new long term space is being acquired or developed. It can also be used when existing space is being refurbished. Figure 2.2 lists the points that need to be considered and the description should be sufficiently detailed for a developer or refurbishment builder to use as a design specification. The document should be kept up to date to take into account the company's changing requirements and new technology.

Evaluation criteria

When the space planning process described above shows that a mismatch of demand and supply will occur, actions must be put in place to address this problem.

The solution also needs to ensure that the building type and location criteria are met.

Firstly, it needs to be established if the requirement is long term or short term. If the new space is to form part of the long term core of the portfolio, it must meet the specification. This may mean that a specific development needs to be initiated if suitable space is not available on the market. If the space is required to meet a short term variation, then the crucial points are to acquire the correct amount of space with a term that fits into the overall strategy.

This is where an understanding of the property market is essential, either by the use of in-house resource or by using a firm of surveyors. Apart from information on the availability of space and future supply, input is required when evaluating the various options.

When looking at the options to provide long term space a financial model needs to be set up which will appraise different options on a consistent basis. In most companies this model would involve looking at the options on a discounted cash flow basis. Discounted cash flow is a method of comparison which assesses how much you need to invest now at an assumed interest rate to pay for future cash flows which will include allowances for inflation. In this way a true comparison can be made between the cost of owning a building or renting one. The model also needs to take into account the different running costs of the various options, any changes in valuation or the periodic cost of refurbishment.

It is probably best to look at all these costs over a 10 year period and discount them back to the present day. This approach is sometimes called life cycle costing, and it can also be used on smaller decisions – eg should a cladding system be installed which may have a higher capital cost than other systems, but with the benefit of lower ongoing maintenance charges?

As with all models, the results will be affected by the economic climate. For example, in a recession the construction cost for a new building could be relatively low – as will the rented option. However, after five years, market changes may lead to disproportionate rental increases.

SPECIFICATION OF STANDARDS

1	Air-conditioning	34	Floor to Ceiling	65	Population
2	Art Programme		Height	66	Postroom
3	Attic Stock	35	Gas Supply	67	Public Address
4	Basement	36	General Decoration		System
5	Beverage Points	37	Generator	68	Raised Floor
6	Blinds	38	Goods Area	69	Reception
7	Bridge Link	39	Gross to Net Ratio	70	Risers & Ducts
8	Caretaker Flat	40	Hairdressing Salon	71	Roof
9	Carpets	41	Hospitality Room	72	Security
10	Ceilings	42	Flammable	73	Security Beacons
11	Cleaner's Facilities		Materials	74	Service Cores
12	Clocks	43	Internal Signs	75	Service Outlets
13	Colour	44	Ironmongery	76	Shops
14	Copy & Printing	45	Kitchen	77	Showers
15	Curtains	46	Kiosk	78	Skin Design
16	Data Connections	47	Ladder Store	79	Soundproofing
17	Disabled Provisions	48	Landscaping	80	Staircases
18	Door Bells	49	Letter Box	81	Storage
19	Doors & Frames	50	Lift Lobbies	82	Telephone and Data
20	Drainage	51	Lifts - Goods		Cabling
21	Electrical Supply	52	Lifts - Passenger	83	Telephone & VDU
22	Emergency Lighting	53	Lightning		Controller Equip
23	Energy Conservation	54	Lightning Protection	84	Toilets
24	Entrances	55	Lock Mechanisms	85	Trolley Access
25	External Signs	56	Medical Room	86	TV Aerial
26	Facade Cleaning	57	Office Equipment	87	Vandalism
27	Fire Detection	58	Partitions	88	Vehicle Parking
28	Fire Exists	59	Paving	89	Visibility
29	First Aid	60	Pipework	90	Wall Types
30	Fixed Offices	61	Planning Grid	91	Waste Disposal
31	Floor Finishes	62	Plant Controls	92	Water Supply
32	Floor Loading	63	Plant Management	93	Windows
33	Floor Slab Design	64	Plantrooms	94	Workshops

(Figure 2.2)

Refurbishment options

A common decision when defining your property strategy is the choice between refurbishing existing property or relocating to a different building. The final decision will often represent a balance of four factors:

- Is there sufficient time available to achieve each of the alternatives?
- Can the current property stand modification to meet business needs?
- What are the capital costs of refurbishment?
- What are the projected running costs compared to the alternatives?

Your current building may not be capable of meeting the demands of future IT installations, for example, or providing the correct working environment to meet your staff expectations.

The capital cost of refurbishment, together with the cost and operational impact of temporary accommodation, may far outweigh the expense of relocating to a purpose designed property. Your running costs in a refurbished building may exceed those for a modern property. Some of these issues are brought into context by considering a case study.

A simple case study

You may be faced with a variety of options when considering the implementation of your strategy. This case study demonstrates the importance of keeping your objectives clearly in mind when looking at the type of options which could be available to you.

Figure 2.3 shows relative example costs of running three different buildings: a new owner occupied property, an older speculative building and a recently constructed speculative building. The older property requires extensive refurbishment to bring it to the same standard as the newer buildings. Figure 2.3 shows that in terms of costs per sq ft, refurbishment may be the most cost effective option. However, in this particular example, the structure is incapable of being adapted to meet the occupational density levels and IT requirements which the new build option might achieve.

Thus in terms of cost per occupant (which in the final analysis is the most appropriate measure of value for money), the refurbished building can prove the most expensive option.

Clearly there are horses for courses and if you have a high space allocation per head you may be advised to take the refurbishment option. The main point in this example is to demonstrate the need to test each of your options carefully against your business objectives.

Some practical points

If you follow the key steps of defining space requirements and specification and then evaluating the various options to meet these requirements, you will have the basis of a sound strategy.

Your property strategy plan should be regularly reviewed. In particular – are the assumptions on staff growth still realistic and what is happening in the property market?

OPERATIONAL PROPERTY COSTS
COST PER SQUARE FOOT

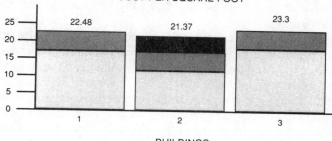

BUILDINGS

EXPENSE CATEGORIES

RENT & RATES   FACILITIES   REFURBISHMENTS

DISC

1	-	2yr Old Owner Occupied Building
2	-	20yr Old Speculative Building
3	-	4yr Old Speculative Building

OPERATIONAL PROPERTY COSTS
COST PER OCCUPANT

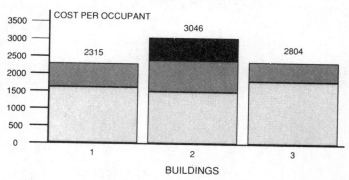

BUILDINGS

EXPENSE CATEGORIES

RENT & RATES   FACILITIES   REFURBISHMENTS

DISC

NB: REFURBISHMENT DEPRECIATED OVER 20 YRS
ALL BUILDINGS ARE AIR CONDITIONED

(Figure 2.3)

It is also worth taking a pessimistic view on most things! For example, timescales are always longer than predicted, costs always seem to escalate and valuations are sometimes too optimistic.

Although many organisations could not justify the cost of an in-house team to handle property strategy, even with a relatively small requirement it is essential to have good communication between the key players. These will probably include a commercial surveyor, solicitor, space planner, quantity surveyor, the firm's accountant and a 'users' input. If these individuals understand the business objectives then a good result should be achieved.

The key to success will depend on the flexibility of your plan. No matter how large or small your company may be, you will need to react quickly to changing circumstances. Large portfolios may benefit from a mix of owned and leased property; all organisations should look for breakpoints in long-term leases. Although your analysis of benefits and costs may clearly justify relocating to new premises, you will not be thanked for overlooking all the headaches which will result from leaving an undisposed building vacant after your move.

Checklist

- The importance of property strategy
  - Frequently the second largest cost
- Strategic space planning
  - Calculate the projected demand, and compare with your supply.
- Specification of long term space
  - Location
  - Building design
- Evaluation criteria
  - Financial modelling
  - Life cycle costing.
- Refurbishment options
  - Business needs versus costs
- Case study
  - Weigh all the issues
- Practical points
  - Regularly review your plan
  - Be wary of optimistic estimates and timescales
  - Agree communication links for key people
  - Retain flexibility

CHAPTER THREE

MANAGING SPACE ——————

In this Chapter we discuss:

- The significance of premises costs
- Formulating a successful strategy
- Evaluating the existing situation
- Focusing on real costs
- Practical steps to adopt
- Office moves
- Total quality environment

The significance of premises costs

Premises costs are usually a close second to staff overheads in the expense picture for most organisations today. Since property-related costs are driven by space allocation it follows that efficient management of your space is therefore key to containing these costs. The real trick is to match your property strategy to the company business plan by understanding the functions and roles of various departments and defining consistent guidelines to allocate space.

When business growth, contraction or steady-state is projected against your guidelines the ideal specification will be defined, and opportunities can arise when a mismatch occurs between availability of space and your requirement. This is when a thorough appreciation of building running costs can help to identify property for disposal or acquisition. Managing space in small businesses is usually more clear cut, but planning ahead will still pay dividends and a known strategy will help with rent/buy and location decisions.

Formulating a successful strategy

Your aim is to develop a strategy based on a set of guidelines for accommodating different departments so that you can achieve optimum usage of your space. You may find it useful to explain current accommodation strategy to senior managers and directors and to outline your thoughts for the future.

This can be achieved through presentations to different groups, and the ensuing discussions will act as a sounding board for various scenarios, help people to understand your general approach, and provide feedback on initial proposals. Most managers will be very receptive to any initiatives for improving working environments and reducing premises costs, and this will help to justify your proposals.

Evaluate the existing situation

The space allocation for your company will depend on a number of disparate factors. Some of the more significant considerations are:

- Business factors
  - Corporate role and image
  - Culture and expectations
  - Location
  - Affordability
  - Growth projections
  - Ratio of staff grades and functions
  - Working practices and attendance patterns

- Other factors
  - Building design
  - Frequency of internal moves
  - Use of IT
  - Storage requirements
  - Existing guidelines and standards
  - Footprint dimensions of furniture system
  - Numbers and sizes of meeting rooms
  - Other facilities such as kiosks or vending
  - Efficiency of space planning

You will find it useful to plot space allocation for each department to clearly show the existing picture. Figures 3.1 and 3.2 give examples for departments A to S.

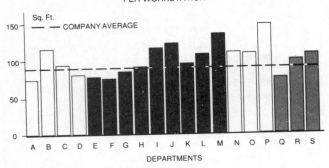

(Figure 3.1)

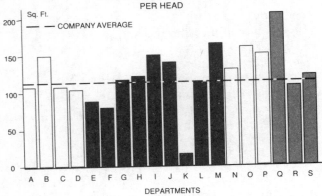

(Figure 3.2)

The plots reflect divisional structure for quick comparison against company averages. Figure 3.1 shows the average amount of workstation space allocated to all the people in different departments and Figure 3.2 shows the average total space occupied, including support space such as meeting rooms, storage areas and circulation space. The data can be refined further as shown in Figures 3.3, 3.4 and 3.5.

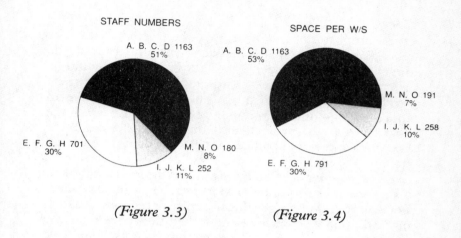

STAFF NUMBERS

A. B. C. D 1163
51%

E. F. G. H 701
30%

I. J. K. L 252
11%

M. N. O 180
8%

(Figure 3.3)

SPACE PER W/S

A. B. C. D 1163
53%

M. N. O 191
7%

I. J. K. L 258
10%

E. F. G. H 791
30%

(Figure 3.4)

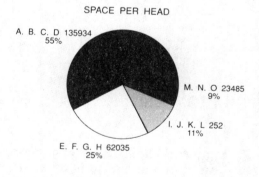

SPACE PER HEAD

A. B. C. D 135934
55%

M. N. O 23485
9%

I. J. K. L 252
11%

E. F. G. H 62035
25%

(Figure 3.5)

Armed with this powerful information you can begin your evaluation, exploring the reasons for different space allocations. By showing your people the cost of providing their facilities you can start to pose some searching questions in departments where the norm is significantly exceeded.

Understand the business plan

It is important that the people vested with the responsibility for space management understand the direction of their company. In other words they should be kept aware of business – and staff – projections, new product initiatives and so on. They should also have an appreciation of the corporate image and culture which the board wishes to project, and broadly understand the functions and work practices of different departments and staff.

Corporate expense budgets will also figure strongly, and a knowledge of corporate property strategy will be needed. For example, if leases are due to expire or be re-negotiated, or if additional space is planned then the space manager needs to know. These and any similar issues will all have an impact on planning.

Focus on real costs

The plots at Figures 3.1 and 3.2 can easily be translated to a cost basis by applying the unit costs derived from adopting the procedures at Chapter 4. This will show the expense pattern for each department and these overheads can be examined in perspective for each profit centre.

Against this background you can begin to consider the need for establishing new guidelines and, together with business plan projections, start to define an overall corporate property requirement.

Agree targets

You will find it advantageous to obtain agreement at senior level for your new space targets and guidelines. Your research on current space standards and costs will add credibility to your proposals and when the benefits are explained you should have no difficulty in justifying your systematic approach.

Make sure that department managers are well aware of corporate actions for new standards when you start to implement your plans. This will ease the way for any measures which may be perceived as slightly radical from a parochial viewpoint. Aim to produce quarterly space reports to keep senior management aware of progress - or the lack of it!

Flexible solutions

Try to retain flexible solutions to respond quickly to changing demands. This could involve the use of layouts which can be quickly altered to meet new requirements and the inclusion of some contingency space. Efficient space management can be like playing three-dimensional chess! You will need a thorough knowledge of the rules, a creative brain and a singular focus on your objectives.

The challenges are constant and the rewards high. The advice on setting guidelines will help you to achieve the flexibility needed to meet these challenges.

Setting your guidelines

The amount of space you allocate to various members of staff should reflect the needs of their job. You may also wish to consider job grades in arriving at your standards, as well as some of the diverse factors listed earlier in this chapter. Your business may require a high ratio of cellular offices compared to open plan workstations, but be prepared to challenge established practices if you are in doubt.

Fixed offices are generally more expensive and less flexible. Point out the additional costs and make your recommendations. This will help your directors or partners to weigh pros and cons.

Open plan factors

After you have completed your review of the existing space allocations across your company you may find that space standards in different departments have significantly diverged over the years. This is not unusual, particularly for organisations using large open plan offices. Your aim is to propose appropriate open plan factors (OPFs) – the average open plan space per workstation in any given area – for departments with similar roles.

The emphasis should be on adequate space for the job, remembering that another 10% will have a similar impact on your bottom line expenses.

Of course, a single OPF will rarely be appropriate but 3 or 4 should cover most eventualities.
For example:

- Secretarial OPF   – 90 sq ft
- Clerical OPF   – 65 sq ft
- Supervisory OPF – 80 sq ft
- Managerial OPF   – 90 sq ft

This demonstrates the 'space for the job' principle: a manager may need more space than his staff for reasons of confidentiality, say, whereas his secretary requires extra space for filing cabinets.

Publish your guidelines after ratification and follow the principles to see benefits accrue. But remember - they are guidelines and not a strait-jacket!

Fixed space

Areas which are permanently partitioned off are usually defined as fixed space. This might include offices, meeting rooms, training facilities and centralised filing areas, for example. It is not uncommon for these facilities to occupy some 25% of the total available space, even for organisations which might consider themselves to be largely open plan in nature. Thus, it is important to consider guidelines for allocating your fixed space as well as for open plan areas.

As with selecting OPFs, you will need to carefully consider functions and roles when defining your standards. Senior directors might have slightly larger offices then non-executive directors and small meeting rooms might be constructed for one-to-one staff meetings while retaining larger rooms for group discussions. Examples of fixed space factors (FSFs) are:

- Senior director office   – 250 sq ft
- Non-executive director office – 150 sq ft

- One-to-one meeting room   – 100 sq ft
- Group meeting room   – 250 sq ft

You should also aim to agree a meeting room to staff ratio.

A similar approach can be applied for training rooms where room size should depend on the number of students on a typical course. When defining storage requirements you should encourage managers periodically to cull files or at least shed archives to less expensive remote storage sites.

Standard layouts

Your OPFs and FSFs will help you to develop standard layouts for various floors and buildings. These layouts should be consistent with building grids, fenestration, air conditioning outlets and lighting as well as the basic footprint of your furniture system.

Standard layouts offer significant advantages over random designs, as Figure 3.6 shows. They provide greater flexibility for reacting to change, reduce the cost of essential internal moves and are easier to manage. They are also aesthetically more pleasing and more conducive to good productivity.

Thus, if people transfer between sections they are familiar with the workstation layout; if whole departments relocate, then layout alterations are minimised; and if additional storage or special areas are required these can be constructed with minimum disruption.

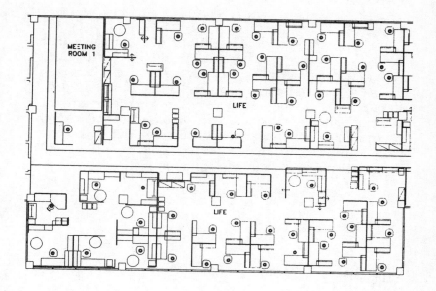

(Figure 3.6)

Contingency

As part of your space rationalisation you should aim to allocate contingency areas adjacent to volatile – or high churn – departments wherever possible. These contingency areas should reflect the size of the department and will allow flexing with a minimum of future disruption. The areas could contain some workstations – built to standard guidelines – with some open areas for use as ad-hoc meeting places, for example.

33

Department locations

You will need a good understanding of the organisation and role of each department to fit the jigsaw together within the constraints of your building envelope. You may choose to centralise departments of like function, with support areas located nearby to reflect workflow patterns. Alternatively, your plans could be based on divisional responsibilities and hierarchical structure. Either way, you will find it advantageous to prepare a list of options and invite your board to ratify the optimum plan.

Benefits

Remember at each stage to outline the potential benefits which your systematic approach to space management will bring. Some of your proposals may seem bureaucratic at first sight but put in the context of tighter control over a major corporate asset then your case will be convincing. Translate reductions in space to a financial saving using your operational cost database. Also try to estimate the added value that standard layouts and contingency space will have in terms of reduced disruption to main core business.

Typically, the cost of each move for standard layouts is about 25% of that requiring a customised design. Line management time is reduced – there is less scope for negotiation – and staff will be immediately familiar with their new location. You will be impressed by the impact on bottom line expenses – and so will your boss.

Some common issues

In line with the increasing profile which space management is taking, there are a number of associated issues which frequently arise. Most of these reflect the realisation that flexible solutions require flexible space management to meet today's business challenges. Some commonly encountered aspects are outlined as follows.

Shared workspace

In departments where staff spend a significant part of their time away from their desks – consulting with clients or at other meetings, for example – you might consider introducing shared workspaces. In this way, space and furniture could be reduced by, say, 30%. Thus, for a department of 100 staff, only 70 work positions would be required – but a word or two of caution.

Firstly, you will need to carefully survey department modus operandi before choosing an appropriate ratio. A pilot scheme would help to establish a realistic figure. Secondly, your voice and data equipment will need to have the flexibility to support the initiative. Staff will need to key their location into PCs and telephones and obtain the correct response. Personal filing can be stored in mobile pedestals or cabinets alongside shared areas.

Telecommuting

Homeworking can also help to reduce your premises costs if significant numbers of staff can successfully operate from their own homes via modem links. This method of working lends itself to all kinds of functions dependent upon automatic data processing. Some central facilities will no doubt be needed to accommodate people when attending appointments at your offices, but if homeworking is a viable option then benefits can be worthwhile.

Shift working

Your company has invested heavily in providing the right accommodation to meet business objectives. But this investment typically lies idle for at least half of the day. Shift working or 'hot desking' could help to reduce property overheads if your business and culture will permit it. In this way the working day can be extended to give, say, a 16 hour per day operating cycle with each shift using the same facilities.

This pattern will significantly reduce your office space requirement, and there could be spin-off advantages too. For example, the extended working day might smooth out peak computer loads and power consumption, helping to avoid exceeding threshold capacities. But do not forget to involve your Personnel Department early on in the decision process – shift working could affect salaries and conditions of employment.

Productivity

It is not always easy to formally relate productivity to environmental conditions. Surveys have been attempted but data gathering is not straightforward. By singling out your people for a survey you can make them feel special, and productivity monitoring can therefore lead to artificial results, certainly over a short period. But few can deny that an efficient office layout and pleasant working conditions will help to motivate your staff, with a corresponding impact on productivity.

Statutory regulations

As well as addressing some of the more obvious health and safety issues in Chapter 10 you will need to check space plans with your local Fire Officer. In particular make sure that your standard layouts are within maximum densities permitted by the British Standards Institution's code of practice on fire precautions. For example, the width of fire escapes may dictate the total number of staff who can be accommodated on each floor of your buildings.

Furniture systems

The footprint of your furniture system – ie a plan view of the area occupied – may affect OPFs, standard layouts and the basic design of your workstations. In some cases this may prove a restrictive factor, constraining the minimum size of your work areas and limiting the occupation density for given floors. Choosing new furniture can also be tricky. Your requirements will influence your choice but some of the factors worth considering are: budgets, systems or conventional design, durability, flexibility and size related to building grid.

Whatever your choice, two things are certain – the cost will be significant and you will live with your decision for some time to come. So evaluate your short-list carefully against your selection criteria. Again, a trial may prove useful before placing your order.

Office moves

After your analysis of department space you may wish to introduce some control measures to minimise the number of internal office moves - or office 'churn' as it is sometimes known. It will be useful to establish the ball-park annual cost of your moves so that your colleagues understand the importance of adequate controls.

Unit costs will vary significantly between different companies and it is not easy to establish common definitions for comparing apples with apples. Be sure to include costs for in-house personnel as well as contractors, telephone and data cabling, additional cleaning and security, and maintenance (eg touch-ups for chipped paintwork and air conditioning adjustments) as well as the more obvious expenses.

You can show churn rates by department, by full time equivalents (FTE), in a similar format to the space utilisation charts at Figures 3.1 and 3.2 in Figure 3.7.

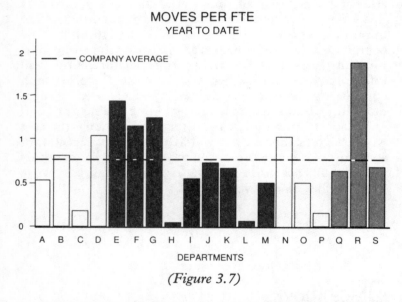

(Figure 3.7)

Office move reports can be made cumulatively on, say, a quarterly basis. As with the space charts, it will be useful to translate the number of moves into costs. This information will probably attract some interesting feedback from your departments and the increased profile should create support for tightened control of internal moves. A good way to achieve this is by introducing an authorisation form which estimates the cost of a requested move, outlines the expenditure year-to-date and requires departmental justification as shown in Figure 3.8.

REQUEST FOR OFFICE REORGANISATION

Project Reference: Date:

1. Details of Requirements

Department: Workstation Moves
                         Required:

Location: Fixed Office Moves:

Co-ordinator: Staff Numbers
                         Proposed/Budget:

2. Reasons For Alterations

A) Property Strategy B) Growth C) Restructure
D) Other

Amplifying Comments:

3. Controls

A) Workstation Moves

- Total budgeted for year:
- Total Company year-to-date:
- Total Department year-to-date:

B) Furniture

- Total Company budget:
- Total expenditure to date:

(Figure 3.8)

4. Space Standards

A) Current Standards: Block Space
Allocated:
Usage area
per head:

B) Proposed Standards: Block Space
Allocated:
Usable area
per head:

5. Costs

A) Building Running Costs : effect on costs at
£x per ft^2:

B) Cost of Reorganisation:

C) Cost of additional furniture and equipment:

D) Cost of building works:

E) Other costs (eg data cabling):

6. Alternatives

Divisional Manager:

Director:

Recommendation by
Facilities Department:

Comments:

(Figure 3.8)

Computer aided design

If you have a large building portfolio then you should consider a computer aided design (CAD) installation. CAD provides many opportunities to work smarter, both strategically and in day-to-day terms. At the higher level an automated system will help you to analyse and understand key data at each stage of the strategic planning cycle.

By presenting your information in a systematic format you will help your directors with corporate decision-making. It will enable you to evaluate options and reach cost effective solutions on the issues affecting office space, running costs and property strategy. At the tactical level the most obvious application for CAD is as an electronic drawing board, but it is also a powerful tool when used as a menu driven database for asset management and budget tracking.

An automated system is quick, accurate, helps to coordinate different disciplines such as data-cabling and furniture layouts, and offers good stock control. There are also some non-quantitative benefits such as increased ability to explore alternative layouts, greater flexibility, better job satisfaction and improved presentation.

There are many systems on the market and your specification will be influenced by some of the factors which affect your general approach to space management outlined earlier in this chapter. In making your selection remember that there are two key requirements: a database for decision making and a design tool. A PC is probably adequate for most applications and you will also need a comprehensive software package. The best way to develop an effective system is to bite the bullet by installing a well proven but relatively inexpensive system to meet your needs.

Total quality environment

Productivity and quality in the workplace are inextricably linked by a single objective: getting it right first time. Quality is about continually meeting customer expectations – providing the service needed to an agreed standard. In this respect staff and not management will usually have the biggest impact on success, and total commitment is pre-requisite.

By definition therefore, a motivated workforce needs to feel involved in all aspects of work – including the design of the work environment – to achieve high productivity. Few will deny that a happy, well motivated workforce aligned to a single business aim – and sharing in business success – will be productive.

But there are two sides to the coin. Productivity and quality are also about efficiency: providing the right service at the right time but also at the right cost. One of the dangers of active participation in workstation design is that staff expectations may be raised beyond the levels of affordability.

The key is often to paint the higher level picture to staff by placing operating costs in perspective against productivity – in other words, greater involvement. As we have seen, premises costs may be the second largest expense after staff costs for many organisations, and the single biggest cost driver here is space allocation.

Simple graphic presentations showing the impact of space guidelines and department allocations on the bottom line will help staff to understand the underlying need for effective design. In this way their involvement will be constructive and help to achieve a truly productive workplace.

Finally, it is worth emphasising that the common theme throughout your space management should be to provide a total quality environment – to construct facilities which take account of people factors and productivity as well as straightforward economics. Indeed these aspects are probably synonymous: as costs and expectations rise you must aim to deliver not only an efficient solution, but also an intelligent one.

Checklist

- Formulate a successful strategy
  - Evaluate the existing situation
  - Understand your business plan
  - Focus on real costs
  - Agree targets
  - Retain flexible solutions

- Setting your guidelines

  Agree:
  - Open plan factors
  - Standard layouts
  - Fixed space
  - Contingency
  - Department locations
  - Benefits

- Some common issues

  Consider:
  - Shared workspace
  - Telecommuting
  - Shift working
  - Productivity
  - Statutory regulations
  - Furniture systems
  - Office moves
  - Computer aided design
  - Total quality environment

CHAPTER FOUR

COST CONTROL ─────────────

One of the key roles of a facilities manager is to deliver the correct service at the correct time and quality, and at the correct cost. Since property and service costs are rapidly becoming one of the highest expenditure areas for many companies, they require a cost control system equal to their significance. This Chapter explains the basis of good cost control and covers:

- Budgeting
- Life cycle costing
- Forecasting and action plans
- Expenditure tracking
- Capital works

The cost control cycle

Cost control is not an isolated procedure but a series of steps, starting at budget setting and running through to final accounting.

The key to good control is forecasting in sufficient time to enable cost control actions to be implemented. These steps are illustrated in Figure 4.1.

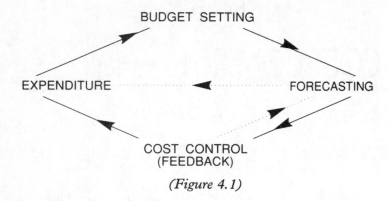

(Figure 4.1)

However, cost control is not about bottom line decision making; good cost control is about controlling the parts that make up the whole.

Budgeting

The cost control process commences with budgeting, which in itself is an art. However, there are some basic steps that can be taken to reduce the guesstimated nature of many budgets. These steps are noted below and illustrated in Figure 4.2. Whilst this may be a cumbersome task at the outset it will pay dividends in years to come and will assist in forecasting.

Step 1   Identify the main components of expenditure i.e. rent, rates, service charges, capital projects, cleaning etc.

Step 2   Identify sub-components, eg on cleaning you might easily find:
Regular daily cleaning
Special cleaning
Carpet cleaning

BUDGETING FOR PROPERTY EXPENSES

STEP 1	STEP 2	STEP 3	STEP 4				STEP 5	STEP 6	
SPECIFICATIONS			COST DRIVERS						
Main Expense Headings	Sub Headings	Client Spec	Quantity	Quality	Time	Cost	Base Cost £	Contin-gency £	Total Cost £
Rent									
Rates									
Service									
Charges									
Cleaning	Daily	To meet client req'ments	Area	To meet client req'ments	1 per day	Inflation			
	Special		Area		100 per day				
	Carpets		Area		4 per year				
	Windows		Area		3 per year				
	Wages		Staff No.s		Hrs				
	Consumables		Orders		-				
	Blinds		Area		1 per year				
	Trade Waste		Volume		1 per week				
Utilities									
Floral									
Security									
Office									
Moves									
Leasehold									
Maintenance:									
• Building									
• Mechanical									
• Electrical									
• A/C									
• Lifts									
TOTAL									
CAPITAL									
Building Projects									
Mechanical Projects									
Equipment									
Furniture									
Fixtures /Fittings									
TOTAL									

(Figure 4.2)

47

Window/cladding cleaning
Consumables
Blind cleaning
Waste clearance

Step 3 Identify the specification for each. In considering the specification you should consider whether the end-user/client requires this level of specification or whether there are parts of the specification which could be reduced, even stopped or enhanced.

Step 4 Identify the drivers of cost such as floor space, contractual terms, inflation, frequency of services, etc. Once the drivers have been identified, collate your latest views on these and adjust your budget to reflect their influence. It is worth keeping a record of your cost driver assumptions as these will become key to forecasting any likely changes to your budget.

Step 5 There are a variety of ways to establish the costs for each sub component:

- previous year's actual expenditure and inflation.
- contract negotiations/tender.
- contractors asked to analyse their quotations in detail.
- analysis by external consultancies.

Step 6 Parts of your budget will be totally reactive to certain events occurring. Where this is the case, again make assumptions on best available information. Include in this section contingency allowances for worst case scenarios. Previous data is always useful on these types of expenditures to enable trends to be analysed which in turn should help reduce the reactive nature of the expenditure.

Step 7 Having now compiled the budget and submitted it for approval, the inevitable request for cuts is made. Where this situation occurs, do not cut arbitrarily but make reasoned judgements on the cost driver assumptions and adjust them to suit.

Last but not least, the point in time at which your budget is prepared is clearly important, ie the further away the budget setting is from expenditure the greater the risk to that budget. However, having followed the steps outlined, your ability to easily identify change will make the forecasting process that much more accurate.

Life cycle costing

At this stage it may be necessary to consider various options to achieve your budget. In some cases there is a tendency to make short term gains, without the benefit of knowing the longer term impact. You can mitigate against this situation through the use of discounted cash flows.

There are a variety of ways in which capital outlay can be measured against continuing revenue expenses, all of which evolve around the use of net present value calculations. This is usually referred to as Life Cycle Costing. It is the process by which the true cost of a particular option can be ascertained over a period of time. It enables initial capital costs and on-going running costs to be reduced back to present day values to compare the long term cost of different alternatives.

The construction industry is developing life cycle costings to measure the performance costs of various materials and products. There are, however, some limiting factors:

- This method of appraisal is approximate and should be subject to sensitivity analysis.

- The interest rates (or horizons) used in the calculation can vary from internal rate of return to estimated RPI.

- The period over which the analysis is carried out should be limited to a maximum of 10 years.

- The effects of not maintaining materials or products in accordance with manufacturers' instructions in some cases is unknown.

Despite the above limitations, this approach does give an order of costs for various options and as such can be extremely useful in determining cost strategies. It should be implemented for all major capital spends.

Forecasting

As a key element of cost control, forecasting relies on good communication both written and verbal, as well as establishing within the budgets a series of cost driver assumptions. It is the monitoring of these cost driver assumptions that will inevitably lead to good forecasting.

However, from a pragmatic view you will not want to spend endless hours tied up in accounting administration. To reduce the administration you should try to eliminate those elements of the budget which, for all intents and purposes, will remain 'fixed' – eg rent where there are no reviews due in the year and costs which are contracted/or committed. This leaves the 'variable' constituents which in the main will be subject to variations caused by a change to the cost driver assumptions: hence the need to monitor pro-actively the cost drivers.

Cost control actions

Having re-forecasted you are now able to establish whether the budget is capable of being sustained; if it is not then corrective action is required. This action can take the form of arbitrary cuts in services, deferment/cancellation of work, or the implementation of a proactive action plan, eg agreed reduction in services and alternative options to perform the services.

Referring back to the cleaning costs example in Step 2, you may decide to revise the content of your daily cleaning specification and reduce some items to an alternate-day basis, or reduce window cleaning frequency from six to four times each year.

It is clearly desirable to implement an action plan where the effects have already been calculated. Deferment means that the service/work still has to be performed and its deferment may impair the running of the business, or worse – becomes an inflated 'fixed' cost for the following year. For example, deferring carpet repairs could lead to premature replacement of badly worn carpets on health and safety grounds.

From a cost control view point, fixed costs are difficult to avoid in the short term and leave little or no room for manoeuvre. However, from a forecasting point of view they are useful in firming up the committed expenditures.

Fixed costs should be dealt with at a strategic level, eg a decision to dispose of a property or a move to sublet space.

One of the idiosyncrasies of property related expenditures is the need to plan ahead. Very few expenses can be curtailed over-night and the use of a three year rolling forecast helps to hone a strategic property plan.

The main tool for determining whether corrective action is necessary is the cost report (Figure 4.3). Clearly from a management view point the 'reason for difference' is essential, in order to implement the appropriate action in the right areas.

EXAMPLE COST REPORT

EXPENSE HEADING	BUDGET £,000s	LATEST FORECAST £,000s	PREVIOUS FORECAST £,000s	DIFF. £,000s	VARIANCE AGAINST BUDGET £,000s	REASONS FOR DIFF.	ACTION REQUIRED	ANTICIPATED VULNERABILITIES OR SAVINGS £,000s	
Rent									
Rates									
Service Charges									
Cleaning	320	340	340	0	20	Special Cleans	Review Spec	Review	(20)
Utilities									
Floral									
Security									
Office Moves									
Leasehold									
Maintenance:									
• Building									
• Mechanical									
• Electrical									
• A/C									
• Lifts									
TOTAL									

(Figure 4.3)

In addition a good cost report should make provisions for anticipated savings/reduction and vulnerabilities, and for actions which may only be tentative but if implemented would impact upon the budget. For example, the imposition of new legislation for VAT or health and safety reasons could prove a budget risk for the facilities manager.

Expenditure tracking

Whilst details of expenditures do not prevent budget overruns they are useful for using in analysis at budget setting stages. Therefore, careful coding of invoices and subsequent logging either in central accounts or as a separate administration function will be helpful.

A diverse range of facilities management activities requires a comprehensive span of control based on good communication, regular reporting and careful performance monitoring. You will need to agree service levels with your 'clients' – perhaps your partners or department heads; plan your expenditure within the corporate budget; and set up a series of key indicators to ensure your targets are met. You will probably find that a monthly frequency of reporting is better than a quarterly basis. This will enable you to take timely remedial action to address any shortfall in service levels, or to adjust uncommitted expenditure to achieve annual budgets.

As with most control systems, the essence of a successful procedure is to keep your reports simple and straightforward. Your time will be well spent in initial selection of the most appropriate key performance indicators and report formats. This will enable accurate and powerful facilities management data to be 'viewed at a glance' and provide you with a sound foundation to deliver the right service at the right cost and the right time.

Capital works

During the life of a building there will be times when a major capital expenditure is required, such as a refurbishment or plant replacement. Capital expenditures, as with all costs, are influenced by time, quality and costs. By examining each of these in turn the determining factors can be seen.

Time

There are two aspects which will be influenced by time. Firstly, the timing of when the spend will occur, and secondly the length of time for carrying out the works.

The timing of when the expenditure will occur will probably be determined by one of the following:

- Budget availability
- Staff re-organisation
- New lease/additional space
- No alternative (eg reactive).

The affordability aspect is probably the greatest influence as there is always pressure to keep major capital spends as low as possible. This pressure can result in deferment of the spend in favour of increased maintenance costs. This is not necessarily incorrect provided that there is full knowledge firstly of the cost implications for additional maintenance, and secondly when the back stop date is going to occur. Invariably most major works will have a period of opportunity within which the works can take place.

The back stop date can be determined through regular

condition surveys, as well as examination of life expectancy which will normally be noted in the maintenance manuals. The window of opportunity within which the works have to be carried out is created through other factors such as a major staff relocation, or where the business constrains works to long weekends, for example.

Clearly then the timing of the spend has to be controlled, and this can only effected through a capital works programme, which can be a 5-10 year rolling programme. The most important aspect of the programme will be the identification of the 'window of opportunity' within which the works can be carried out. The absence of such a programme is likely to result in a 'no alternative' position which invariably will not sit well with other influencing factors.

The duration of the works on site can be determined to suit the needs of the client. One of the major factors here will be the effect on business, which should be kept to a minimum. The most likely outcome, depending on the type of works, is a phased approach. This may cost more in direct costs but is likely to yield significant benefits.

Quality

The qualitative aspects of any capital costs are determined by the specification level and, as with any expenditure, there will always be a range of options available. Some options may be influenced by time such as purchasing proprietary units instead of site manufacture.

It is only through detailed examination of the options that the best value for money solution will be found. This process is sometimes referred to as value engineering.

Again a longer term view should also be taken to ensure that the right quality is being achieved. For example, a new carpet with a design life of 10 years would not be good value when the occupation of the building will be for only five years.

Costs

Your capital costs can be split into two main categories - direct costs, and indirect costs. A major spend on an existing occupied building can easily have indirect costs amounting to considerably more than the direct costs. This is particularly so where decanting of staff is required, or duplicated IT systems are needed.

In order to arrive at the budget for capital expenditure it is important to breakdown the elements of the project into easily identifiable categories. This includes the indirect expenses as well.

Once these basic costs have been established then the effect of the time and qualitative options can be considered. It may also be worth considering at this point the effect of capital allowances, as this may have a bearing on the specification of the works. Once an option has been selected then detailed firming up of the costs can take place.

With each element becoming a sub-budget in its own right, the overall budget for the project can be established. It is worth at this stage producing a comprehensive specification/budget which will act as the client brief. This can then be used as the base document from which all variations can be measured.

Checklist

- Budgeting
  - Identify:

    Main expenditure components
    Sub-components
    Specifications aligned to end user requirements
    Cost drivers
    Contingency allowances on reactive spends

  - Take reasoned judgements to reduce budgets to meet affordability; never reduce budgets arbitrarily.

- Life cycle costing
  - Approximate method of appraisal
  - Interest rates may vary
  - Best kept to five year period
  - Requires sound assumptions
  - Despite limitations, LCC can be a useful tool

- Forecasting
  - Monitor cost drivers and their effect on budgets
  - Identify fixed and variable expenditures
  - Consider three year rolling forecasts

- Cost control actions
  - Establish a cost report and publish it
  - Cost overruns should be negated with considered action plans

- Expenditure tracking
  - Useful for analysis and the following year's budget setting exercise
  - Set key indicators relating to agreed service levels
  - Monitor performance

- Capital works
  - Identify timing and duration of project

- Examine the range of options for detailed specification
- Build up sub-budgets to arrive at overall picture

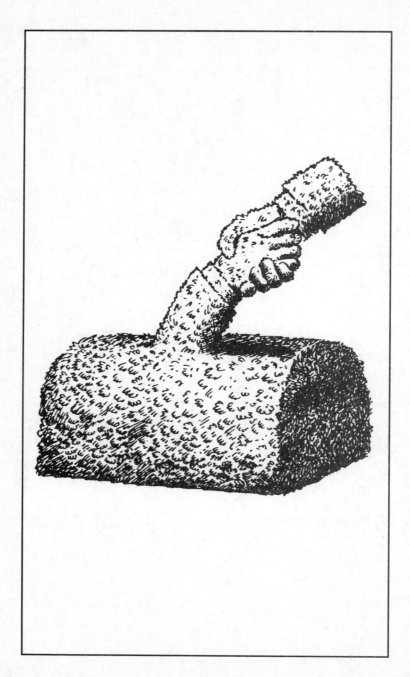

CHAPTER FIVE

THE MANAGEMENT OF OUTSOURCING

In this Chapter we look at the typical issues associated with placing contracts for services not directly connected with the main core business. Outsourcing, as this practice has become known, is often used as a synonym for the global term 'facilities management'. This is not the case.

Outsourcing of contracts is merely one tool or strategy available to the person controlling the overall facilities management for the company. For instance, a company may choose not to outsource at all, but to directly employ and control staff on support services such as cleaning, building maintenance and security. This could be for a number of reasons, such as company culture, location or commercial security.

The issues covered are:

- Typical contracted services
- Organisation of contracted services
- Purchasing skills
- Working with contractors
- Contractor selection
- Specification setting
- Initial contact and short-listing
- Contractor performance
- Single source supply

Typical contracted services

Depending on the range of responsibilities under the control of the facilities manager the more common contracted services are likely to be:

- cleaning
- security
- landscaping maintenance
- mechanical and electrical services (maintenance)
- mechanical and electrical services (projects)
- catering (including vending)
- building maintenance (small works)
- building maintenance (major works)
- property rent and rate reviews
- acquisitions and disposals
- pest control
- waste clearance
- furniture maintenance
- office moves (labour)
- lift maintenance

Other services could include:

- reception staff
- switchboard staff
- health and safety consultancy
- signage production
- photocopiers
- vehicle management
- premises consultancy
- disaster planning back-up
- printing

The range is extremely varied and the above list is by no means comprehensive. For instance, the management of information technology could be included, although this is often considered to be a specialised area of facilities management and constitutes a sector in its own right. What it demonstrates however is the significance of contract management within the facilities management function — hence the need to have a good understanding of how to maintain a tight control over the expenditure incurred and the quality of service provided.

Organisation of contracted services

Most facilities managers will have a significant proportion of their budget in contracted-out services, as much as 90% in some industries, so a good understanding of contracting principles and the effective organisation of contracts is essential.

Outsourcing has almost grown into an industry in its own right. Security and cleaning companies are good examples. Why should this be? In recent years organisations have begun to think more in terms of their core business, to create a sharper commercial awareness and to slim down expensive overheads or 'soft costs'.

Each organisation will have its own definition of what constitutes core and non-core business and this will dictate which elements of the operation remain under direct staff control and those put out to contract. The issue of control, or lack of it, when placing contracts outside the organisation can create feelings of risk or uncertainty. This should not be the case, as a well managed contract will be just as reliable as an in-house managed function, as long as good selection, specification setting and performance monitoring is carried out.

The evolution of managing service contracts has created four basic categories of contract management. These are:

- Dispersed
- Centralised
- Partial grouped or 'bundling'

- Total outsourced

Fig 5.1 shows the principal structuring of each type.

Dispersed

This is the organisationally immature end of contract management, although for some organisations the arrangement may be appropriate. The contracts are controlled by various managers within an organisation who historically may have an interest in particular areas. For instance, the personnel manager may look after the catering contract as it is seen as part of the employee benefits package and the health and safety consultancy contract.

The office manager would look after the photocopier or reprographics services contract, the internal plants contract, furniture contract and office cleaning contract. This would leave the engineering manager or equivalent controlling contracts for services such as mechanical and electrical services, building maintenance, landscape maintenance, lift maintenance, factory cleaning, pest control and so on.

Centralised

Centralising the control of service contracts has become fairly commonplace for many organisations in all industry sectors. This allows a uniform approach to administration, supplier selection and monitoring of performance. Responsibility and accountability is focused, therefore problems are more easily resolved.

The manager responsible, who may go under various titles depending on size of organisation or industry sector (facilities manager, contracts manager, services manager, works engineer, administration manager, office services manager, etc) will often have directly employed subordinates controlling a number of the contracts. The

THE FOUR BASIC CATEGORIES OF CONTRACT MANAGEMENT

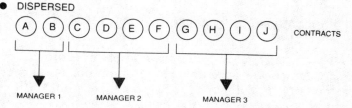

- DISPERSED

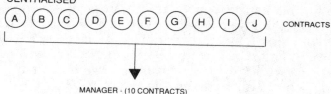

- CENTRALISED

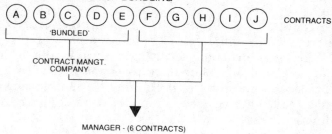

- PARTIAL GROUPED or "BUNDLING"

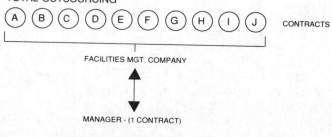

- TOTAL OUTSOURCING

(Figure 5.1)

person will often have other non-contracted duties such as space planning, internal health and safety issues, messenger services, switchboard operation and so on.

Partial grouped or 'bundling'

This normally occurs when the number of contracts under management become unwieldy for one person or section to control. For instance, if we take the contract review process as an example. An organisation with say 27 service contracts covering everything from security and cleaning to lift maintenance and courier transport working on an average three year contract period, will have to review around nine contracts a year. That is one every six weeks. Given that the review process for one contract alone can take six weeks or more, this means the process is a full-time job regardless of any other responsibilities.

Grouping contracts or 'bundling' as it has become known puts a number of contracts under the management of one supplier.

A common grouping can be cleaning, security and catering, three of the more labour intensive services. This development has come about in two ways - the desire of some contracting companies to expand their range of services and make use of more effective site management and clients wanting fewer points of contact and reduced administration.

Total outsourcing

This takes strategic 'bundling' one stage further and puts all service contracts under the direct management of a facilities management company. The internal facilities manager (or equivalent title) creates a 'partnership' with the outsourced company and enjoys one point of contact, one invoicing system, and can often reduce the in-house costs of administering the range of contracts. Of course there is always the risk of having 'all your eggs in one basket', but if the selection process has been carried out properly and appropriate controls are adopted any risk can be reduced to an operationally acceptable level.

Total outsourcing *does not* mean that contracts have to be carried out by one company. In fact, given the range of services required – certainly by large organisations – it is highly unlikely that one company can supply the total range required. However, it does mean that one company can *manage* the range of services specified on your behalf as either individual contracts for each service or bundled to whatever extent is appropriate.

Purchasing skills

If you are fortunate enough to have access to an internal purchasing department who are proactive to your needs and fully understand the value of supportive purchasing (managing money and contracts) – use them, right from the start. Not only will they be another pair of hands on the job, but they will steer you away from some of the common pitfalls in selecting a contracted service.

Do not believe that a purchasing professional who knows a lot about purchasing and little about maintenance, will not be able to help. By working together you will secure benefits or minimise risks that you may not have achieved on your own – an obvious point perhaps, but one that can be overlooked or ignored.

However, not every facilities manager will have the luxury of a purchasing department to call on, especially in the smaller business, so the following sections will help with the main points to consider when looking to appoint a contractor. A useful guide to pro-active purchasing is 'Are you Managing Purchasing?' by Malcolm Jones, which is one of the Allied Dunbar Good Management Practices series.

Working with contractors

The amount of effort that is placed on working with contractors should be relative to the value and sensitivity of the business to be placed. Additionally, you should consider whether you are placing a once-off contract, following which the relationship will end, or whether the contract is the start of a long-term relationship. Some of your most critical or visible services will obviously benefit from the employment of people you can work with for a long time. Also, the effort and cost in changing contractors (say every year) can be considerable.

Consider the workload you are building up for yourself in you go the market every 12 or even 24 months, on say an average portfolio of 12 contracts. In addition, contractors will not see your company as long-term viable business and will only invest a commensurate amount of effort and goodwill.

Try to space out contract review periods and selection projects to achieve an even workload throughout the year. Having all contracts running from January to December is a recipe for disaster.

Contractor selection

Do not be restricted by your own knowledge! A catering manager in a large financial organisation knew of four catering contract companies in the area large enough to be considered for his contract. With assistance from the in-house purchasing department a further five were found and the eventual winner of the business was not one from the catering manager's known four. Even if you are working on your own cast your net beyond your current (more limited than you may admit) knowledge.

Here are a number of points to consider in the selection process.

- Trawl the market in a professional manner, sending contractors a detailed questionnaire on themselves and the services they provide.
- Remove the 'three quotes' barrier by giving everyone in the field an opportunity to respond.
- Concentrate on the quality aspects of performance which are measurable (product, paperwork, service/delivery standards) and set out how you want them to respond.
- Provide contractors with information on your own company.
- Give contractors a set amount of time in which to respond (be firm on this, it is their first test of delivered service).
- Investigate individual contractor trading viability through a recognised agency or perhaps via a bought in on-line system.
- Analyse the information they provide and the way they provide it, and categorise the contractors, negotiate on the component parts to optimise the contract.
- Let contractors know if they have been unsuccessful or have failed to impress and why, if appropriate.
- Remove assumptions about abilities by testing them out, getting them to perform, if possible.

This approach should help you to source new areas and keep existing contractors aware that they cannot afford to be complacent about your business. Listed below are the key stages of selecting a contractor and building a relationship which will ensure confidence that agreements will be met.

Specification setting

In theory, specification setting is simple. It's a straightforward case of someone providing a product or service to meet your requirements. You know what you want, so it's just a case of telling the provider and that's the end of it. Unfortunately, it is not as easy as that in practice.

Some of the pitfalls can be outlined very quickly by use of this simple example. One of your responsibilities is to ensure your organisation's windows are cleaned. Arrangements are made for a local window cleaning firm to do the job once a month at an agreed price. Potentially, that is the end of the story – practically it could be the start of problems. For instance:

- The ground floor, of five storeys, seems to get dirtier than the upper floors due to soil splash-back and proximity to a road. What about a more frequent service for the lower levels?
- The cladding used on the building is susceptible to marking from certain agents. No one has told the window cleaners and they unfortunately use the wrong chemicals to remove some long standing accumulations. The cladding now requires remedial work. Who pays?
- The glass revolving door and side panels at reception do not get cleaned. The window cleaners thought this was the general office cleaner's responsibility.

- A sensitive R & D department does not want its internal glass cleaned out of hours whilst nobody is around. This was not made clear to the contractors.
- The contractors are seen not using the safety equipment provided from the roof cradle system. What are the legal and health and safety implications?
- Skylights are not cleaned as these are not considered to be windows by the contractors. You believe they are windows.
- The contractors complain that they have not been paid within 21 days. . . . Your company's payment cycle is 28 days, and so on.

From this simple example it can be seen that the need for a detailed specification is of paramount importance if the two parties are to work together and achieve a good working relationship which provides a quality service at the appropriate price.

Establish the key factors

It will never be possible to pin down every eventuality within the legalised confines of a specification. Nor is it truly desirable, as the resultant document would resemble a contractual version of 'War & Peace', frightening off most contractors or becoming a procedural millstone around all parties necks.

However, the factors in delivering a service or product which are of critical importance to your organisation must be covered. This will help you and the provider. You need to consider which factors are key in providing the service. The more common ones are:

Time
- When is the service to be delivered?
- Frequency?
- Any restrictions?
- How will 'ad hocs' or emergency call outs be specified?

Staff
- Who is to provide the service?
- Qualifications needed?
- Appearance
- Is security vetting applicable?
- Define the site or sites
- Any restrictions?
- Variations

Procedural detail
- Agreed procedures to be adopted
- Areas to be covered
- Equipment to be inspected or used.
- Checklists to be used
- Appropriate technology
- Training required
- Agreed quality standards
- Performance measurement

Safety
- Any specialised requirements
- Legal obligations
- Training in local procedures
- Equipment/materials to be used/not used
- Reporting of defects/hazards/accidents etc

Security
- Observation of local regulations
- Is security vetting applicable?
- Restrictions on working areas

Management information
- Cost indices
- Checks on service provided
- Regular reports available
- Key data reports available
- Exception reporting

Cost
(May be part of overall contract detail).
- Payment periods
- Authorisation procedures

- Identified rates
- Cost initiatives

Self monitoring

Establishing a tight, yet not overwhelming, specification is the basis for an almost self monitoring system of contract management. Facilities Managers will often be controlling a large number of contracts, either directly or through an outsourcing organisation, so the need for these to be self monitoring or largely trouble free is essential. To achieve this three ingredients are required.

- a well understood specification (with supporting contract)
- an effective management reporting system
- a streamlined administration system

The last two cannot be achieved, or will become ineffective, if the specification is not in place and does not reflect the requirements of the organisation.

Initial contact

Once the specification of the service has been decided and the decision to contract out made, you can make initial contact with contractors.

Your initial contact list can come from:

- Your known preferred contractors
- A manufacturer/dealer/trade listing
- Literature specifically produced to list suppliers of products/services,
- Referrals

You should avoid making contact with contractors with whom you have no intention of dealing. This can only extend the contractor selection exercise unnecessarily, and lead to lack of enthusiasm during potential meetings.

You might consider not dealing with a contractor because of problems in the past, such as personality clashes, assumptions that they cannot meet your requirements, or negative feedback from other users. These are all areas which might not necessarily be the fault of the contractor, and by removing him early in your selection process you may be missing a trick.

Once the initial list has been drawn up, you can make contact with the contractors. There are obviously various ways to do this – by telephone, in face-to-face meetings and in writing. The latter is preferable and more efficient at this stage.

Provide each contractor with an identical specification and list of questions. Not only does this ensure ease of vetting when reading their responses, but fair treatment of all contractors involved is seen by all concerned.

Contractor vetting

The time involved in vetting contractors with the objective of selecting the right one can vary considerably. You may decide that the initial response to your specification is enough for you to make a decision.

Alternatively, you may decide that the duration, value and sensitivity of the contract, together with the requirements of the work warrant a higher level of vetting.

Does the contract require the provision of a service to your company over a considerable time period, say several years? If so, you need to be confident that the contractor will still be around. So ask yourself:

- What is the financial position of the contractor?
- What other contracts does he have?
- What are his plans for the future?
- Is he in a position that he could be bought/sold and what would the effect be on your contract?
- Does he rely on substantial support from a third party (ie, manufacturer) and what if this support is withdrawn?
- What contingencies/disaster back up can the supplier provide?

You also need to know the effect your contract will have on the contractor and where you will be placed as a customer if your contract value is a high percentage of the contractor's turnover – will he be able to handle it?

What if the contractor employs additional staff or invests in additional equipment if he obtains your contract? How will that affect him if you terminate or do not renew the contract?

Conversely, what if your potential contract value is a small percentage of the turnover? Will larger customers take priority?

If you intend to reduce your initial contracts to a short-list, you will need to consider how competitive they are, and to what degree each contractor is prepared to meet your contract terms and conditions. Does the contractor contractually guarantee his service level? How long will prices remain fixed and are there any hidden costs?

It may be necessary, given the nature of the contract, to consider such lengthy criteria. It is always advisable to create a checklist for testing the sensitivity and value of a contract.

Short-listing

Your 'short-list' of contractors may contain the same number as originally contacted, if they have all responded well, or a reduced number following vetting and elimination. The short-list should include those with whom you would be confident about entering into a contract. Meetings would then be arranged for the service, price and contract negotiations.

Your final chosen contractor would be the one offering the best 'value'. This might not be the contractor offering the lowest price if, say, for this you will receive a product and service at the lowest end of the scale (eg, barely meets the technical specification and can just about meet the service criteria). You may prefer a contractor who, for just a slightly higher price, has a far more attractive service.

It is most important that you understand the concept of good all – round value. Once a contractor agrees to a contract, then he really must meet it. The result should be a good service at an acceptable price.

Contractor performance

Most of the tangible evidence of your service to the organisation, as a facilities manager, will come from the provision of a product or service delivered by a contractor. Even if you employ a large number of in-house staff on these services, the performance monitoring principles set out in this section will still apply.

The effective management of contractors is therefore essential to the success of most facilities managers, so it is not safe to assume that once a contract is in place you can leave it confident that the original requirements will always be met.

We all know of the common situations where security guards are not fully trained, cleaners miss workstations, maintenance engineers sign inspection registers without inspecting the equipment and so on. Any number of things can contribute to a gradual deterioration in service from the contractor.

Measurement

There are various methods of measuring contractor performance, but it all comes down to the consistency with which the contractor meets the terms of the contract. It is therefore essential that the original contract clearly defines the service level you require and the way in which that service will be measured.

Feedback should be encouraged and poor performance acted upon immediately. The feedback mechanism and an agreed period of review dates will provide you with the chance to build up a dialogue with your contractor.

It is important to do this soon after commencement of the contract so that a pattern of meetings and feedback reviews is quickly established as the way in which you wish to work. It is no good 'suffering in silence' and then holding an annual review meeting with the contractor at which you tell him for the first time that his service has been poor.

Measurement criteria

In providing a service there are a number of elements that can create measurement criteria:

- Physical evidence that the service has been carried out.
- Clear technical specification.
- Accuracy and timeliness of delivery.
- Absence of complaints from clients/users.

- Pro-active response and planning.
- Clear paperwork produced within an agreed number of days after delivery.
- Ability to resolve the problems within specified time periods.

If specific criteria are identified against which you monitor performance, beware that they do not involve you in a lot of unnecessary administration. Make your measurement benchmarks, clear, simple and unambiguous.

Ideally you should identify a method that is self measuring, can be checked with minimal effort and is immediately apparent to the client and reported directly to the contractor.

Reviews

Once you have passed the early days of a contract and the service is flowing as required, a good way of maintaining contact is to hold regular review sessions. These can be monthly, quarterly or half yearly, depending on the complexity of the contract.

The regular meetings can provide an opportunity to review issues from the previous period, outline what is happening in your own company and discuss future plans and other business opportunities if applicable. You should then discuss cost-savings ideas that could work for both companies, negotiate the next contract period and identify any concerns held by either party.

An overall benefit of regular review sessions is that potential problem areas are identified before they become serious, while the contractor is directly motivated. You should aim to build a good working relationship where either you or the contractor contact each other quickly if any problems arise.

Addressing success/failure

It is as important to address a contractor's success as well as his failure. All too often you can jump on the failure and take success for granted.

If a contractor is successful in maintaining agreed service levels and this generates positive feedback from your client(s), he should be told this in order to show that this is the type of customer reaction you want to see. Remember, good, poor or indifferent contractor performance will reflect upon you. If you are responsible for the cleaning contract and a person's area is not cleaned properly who will get the complaint call? More than likely, you.

If a contractor begins to fail in his obligations, look for reasons why this is happening. You may be able to help resolve the problems.

Often the hardest part of a facilities manager's job is dealing with poor contractor performance. However, with good initial contractor selection and a well documented supply service history, this should be rare.

If the matter cannot be resolved, then business to the contractor should either be gradually reduced (if possible) and an alternative contractor brought on or an instant break made. Whichever decision is taken it should be done clearly and professionally, with no room for misunderstanding about the original problem or the action taken.

Single source contractor

In recent years there has been a move towards single source supply in the facilities management field. This has followed the pattern of large retail or manufacturing businesses who sometimes rely on one supplier for a critical product or component. This is usually achieved after a very long commercial courtship and both sides know exactly what is required and expected.

There can be a high degree of risk but there can be significant advantages as well. One thing is common – a single source supply contract must be extremely well set up and managed for it to be effective. Anything less will end in disaster.

It is fairly common to find one organisation offering all or groups of the following types of service:

- building maintenance
- refurbishment services
- engineering services
- cleaning
- catering
- pest control
- reception staff
- vending facilities
- courier services
- landscaping maintenance
- security
- emergency building services
- environmental audits
- switchboard staff

The decision to put some or all of this type of service into the control of one contractor will depend on a combination of requirements and constraints which will include:

- The current number of individual contracts. For instance, cleaning alone can cover a host of sub-headings all having separate contracts eg, office cleaning, carpet cleaning, window cleaning, blind cleaning, soft furnishing cleaning, kitchen cleans, deep cleans, grounds maintenance, waste clearance and so on.
- The amount of time available for contract management (as opposed to all the other tasks under the facilities manager).
- Costs.
- Vulnerability to risk.
- Available contingency plans.
- Corporate culture.

Advantages

The advantages of using a single contract management company or single source supply include:

- One point of contact for all services (you should have a contract manager on site, if the contract is large enough, to handle communications for the spectrum of services provided).
- Less time in day to day management.
- Less time in reviewing and negotiating contracts (you may have reduced from, say, ten to one).
- Less administration and paperwork.
- More influence over a single contractor.
- The ability to tap into a potential wide range of skills via one source.
- The potential for a good long term working relationship.
- Savings, via reduced senior management positions, on the contracts side and possible economies of scale.
- Flexibility of labour within the contract.

Disadvantages

The disadvantages, although not as long in list form, can outweigh the advantages in terms of weight of importance. However, this will depend on your management structure and vulnerability to risk. The disadvantages can include:

- Reliance on the organisation for a range of very visible services (what happens if they go out of business or receive bad press?)
- Alternative contractors may be limited if your grouping of services is large or unusual.
- Parts of the umbrella service may be expensive compared to alternative suppliers; this could be masked in the overall contract.
- Your contract site manager may not receive the support he needs from his own organisation which can dilute his effectiveness on your contract.

- You may suffer one 'bad apple' service and find it difficult to eliminate as it is bound up in the umbrella service.
- The legal contract may be very complex covering the wide range of services provided.
- You have to 'get on' with the single point of contact (not as trivial as it may sound).

Checklist

- Decide on outsourcing options in line with the overall business objectives of the organisation.
- If you decide on total outsourcing, make sure the selection process for the management company is thorough and approach the working relationship as a partnership.
- Use professional purchasing skills at all times if they are on offer within your organisation.
- At initial contractor selection stage cast as wide a net as possible.
- Pay particular attention to getting the specification correct.
- Only short-list those who you would confidently place the business with.
- Always adopt a measurable contractor performance plan.
- Think carefully before entering a single source supply contract.

CHAPTER SIX

NEGOTIATING AND ACHIEVING A GOOD CONTRACT

A facilities manager may be a first class engineer, surveyor or office services manager, but has probably not been specifically trained in negotiating and constructing a contract. As a large part of many facilities manager's job is probably appointing, monitoring and controlling a number of contract companies a basic understanding of negotiation principles and contracts is essential.

This Chapter covers:

- Competition
- What to negotiate
- Do's and don'ts of negotiation
- Achieving a good contract
- Model contracts

Competition

In trying to achieve your objectives in negotiation, one of the most important strengths is the availability of competition. Competition should be actively encouraged, with contractors being made aware that they are in a competitive situation.

It is amazing how the introduction of competition can create a dramatic change in service levels and price from an existing supplier. For instance, a large household name company was notified by their long- standing maintenance contractor that a price increase would become effective on the next 1 January. Despite several years of good service, the company's requirement was still put out to competitive bidding amongst the contractors competitors. Although the company stayed with the original contractor, the exercise brought many improvements in the service provided, such as:

- better call-out times
- provision for an on-site engineer
- free maintenance periods
- reduction in cost of parts
- payment in arrears instead of in advance
- contract extension - two years
- regular maintenance reports to the client
- quarterly instead of monthly invoices
- contract terms and conditions provided by the customer not the contractor
- prompt payment discounts.
- no price increase; in fact a reduction was achieved

Clearly the market had moved on since the original contract had been established. What would have been unheard of some time ago was now commonplace amongst their competitors.

What to negotiate?

It is all too often thought that the negotiable element of a deal is cost and therefore this is the central issue during negotiation.

Whilst cost is obviously important in any negotiation that involves a financial outlay, a considerable number of other areas can show an advantage and benefit through negotiation; some of them are:

- preferred customer
- price stability
- price variation formula
- prices on sliding scale
- payment terms
- currency/exchange rate
- deferral of price increases
- delivery costs
- delivery dates
- delivery location(s)
- delivery frequency
- insurance
- quality and specification(s)
- quality confidence (new supplier)
- performance guarantees
- reliability
- free samples
- assistance with promotions/trials
- flexibility to changes
- consignment stock
- consolidated stock
- buffer stocks
- collection of rejects/surplus
- emergency response
- buy-back agreement
- lead time/availability
- maintenance/spares/call out

It is too easy to let cost alone dominate negotiations. For instance, a 20% reduction off the industry norm may appear a good result for the Company. However, this becomes irrelevant if the lead time does not match the company's requirements and could end up incurring a cost many times over the initial negotiated discount.

Listening

During all negotiations it is important to listen. Don't let yourself be drawn into a situation where you are continually qualifying the reasons behind your requests. Don't let yourself diversify into areas that do not relate to the points under discussion.

If there are concessions to be made, the person talking the most will make the most!

Assumptions

It is dangerous to make assumptions during negotiations. If you assume something, you are gambling that you are correct in your assumption. As in any form of gambling, from time to time you are going to be wrong.

Also, beware of other people – even so-called experts – trying to influence you with their assumptions. You will often hear these people say:

- 'The contractor will never accept these terms and conditions.'
- 'He's a good contractor, we've been dealing with them for 20 years.'
- '10% is a reasonable price increase in the current climate.'
- 'We've got to let the supplier make a profit.'
- 'There's no way they'll meet these delivery schedules.'

A classic example of tripping over assumptions is demonstrated by the following experience which happened to an office services manager in the brewery industry. He was responsible for the fit-out of new office accommodation including all health and safety and first aid equipment. Using a regular supplier of first aid boxes and medical room kits, he *assumed* the normal 15% off list would apply as he had never been able to better this in the past. It was a considerable spend.

He found out, months later, that the salesman he was dealing with had been a few points short of his incentive bonus target that very month and would have been prepared to offer 25% as a once-off special deal – had he been pushed! He was never asked as it was *assumed* the usual 15% applied.

No matter how obvious something may seem, different assumptions can be made by different people. Always test and challenge every aspect of a deal. Your contractor is going to be skilled at not offering you everything he could – so you must work at getting the best from him on every point throughout the negotiation.

Do's and don'ts in negotiation

DO

- *Prepare*
  Prepare for a negotiation according to the value and complexity of the potential contract. Look for all areas that can provide you with an advantage.

- *Aim high*
  Set your objectives high, which will allow you to be drawn back while still maintaining the advantage.

- *Allow equal opportunities*
  If negotiating with more than one supplier, offer equal opportunities to each to improve the deal. Be fair.

- *Respect confidentiality*
  Respect a supplier's confidentiality and make a supplier

aware that you will not disclose any information received.

- *Deal with decision makers*
  Ensure you are negotiating with someone with the authority to make decisions and agree to your requests.

- *Maintain control*
  Maintain control of negotiations and yourself at all times. Continual questioning will provide you with all the control you need.

- *Be yourself*
  Be yourself, act naturally and enjoy the negotiations. Don't try and add humour if it does not come naturally, but equally don't be over serious. A negotiation is not an interrogation. Remember you are looking for a business partner and both parties should benefit from the resultant deal.

DON'T

- *Give information*
  Don't give a supplier any more information than is required for him to improve his deal. Never disclose the details of one supplier's proposals to another

- *Make assumptions*
  Don't assume anything.

- *Let silence pressure you*
  Don't feel uncomfortable for the supplier. If there is a pregnant pause and it is his turn . . . wait.

- *Give buying signals*
  Never give buying signals such as:
  'When we place the contract . . . '
  'We haven't spoken to anyone else . . .'
  'Yours is a good deal . . . '
  'You are the first person to offer that . . .'

- *Make promises*
  Never make promises that you cannot keep to improve a deal. Don't make statements on future potential

business unless you are sure they are correct, and never guarantee future business on the strength of one contract.

Achieving a good contract

It is not envisaged nor suggested that a facilities manager should be expert at drafting commercial contracts, however a working knowledge of what needs to be covered and how contracts work is essential. Of course, if all goes well, everyone trusts one another, invoices are paid in full and on time, the product is delivered to the right place on time or the service is performed to everyone's satisfaction, no acts of God get in the way, no damage is caused whilst the work is being carried out, there are no disputes . . . etc, etc, etc, . . . then there is no need for a written contract. However, facilities managers tend to operate in the real world!

Your legal department, purchasing department or, in the case of a small company, your organisation's solicitor should be involved in the drawing up of the contract document. They will still require significant input from the facilities manager as it is only you who knows the detail of the service to be bought, the price, the delivery terms, payment terms, liquidated damages arrangements and so on.

Will the standard terms and conditions on the reverse of the purchase order be sufficient? Possibly, but it does depend on the comprehensiveness of the terms and conditions plus the degree of risk involved in the purchase for the organisation. For instance, the purchase of a set of pigeon-hole racks for the post room does not hold the same level of risk (if things go wrong) as the purchase of a lift maintenance service for a 20 storey office block. Assessing the risk can be carried out in different ways. Things to consider:

- A financial limit, eg any spend over £10,000 per single purchase per annum.
- The degree of complexity of the service being provided eg a cleaning service covering routine office cleans, windows, carpets, blinds, waste clearance, special deep cleans, machinery cleans and so on.
- The degree of operational risk, eg a document courier service for a financial institution. The annual value could be low but the implications of regularly missing delivery deadlines could be disastrous.

Model contracts

The use of model contracts is a method of ensuring that all contractual angles are covered and the contract document preparation time is kept to a minimum. Most facilities management purchases, especially services, can be covered by a model contract format.

The term 'model contract' means a standard framework or significant draft which can be used with nil or minor amendments. Models should always be created with legal input, either from an internal legal department or, in the case of smaller organisations, from their commercial solicitor.

Benefits

Model contracts have a number of significant advantages: you do not reinvent the wheel every time a product or service is purchased; a model contract ensures consistency of approach, with adherence to agreed quality standards; and it increases the facilities manager's ability to protect the company contractually.

Caution

However, there are also a few drawbacks to using model contracts. These mainly surround the chances of people acquiring 'tunnel vision' by just filling in the appropriate blank spaces in a model contract, instead of thinking for themselves. Furthermore, as company requirements change and the industrial sector changes, model contracts become out of date.

Both these drawbacks are capable of being addressed without great difficulty. It requires vigilance to assess any opportunities which exist in each situation *before* referring to the model contract.

Not every contractor is happy about accepting model contracts, and any variations requested then become a matter of negotiation.

Format

Model contracts are not a new concept, and are certainly not unique. There are two relevant models to consider:

- Purchase of physical products.
- Purchase of services.

Each individual model represents a list of standard requirements specific to each of the two categories.

For instance, the basic requirements of a physical product contract could contain:

- definitions
- scope
- duration
- risk/property
- purchase price

- contractors obligations
- confidentiality of service
- your company's obligations
- termination
- force majeure
- liquidated damages
- waiver
- assignment
- operational procedures
- jurisdiction
- full specification
- appendices to the contract
- warranties
- service arrangements

Successful model contracts should be written in plain English so that everyone can understand the obligations and implications, they should be fair and reasonable to both parties, and they should lay great emphasis upon the product specification, as no contract, however tight, will protect a loose specification. Therefore everybody needs to take care.

A common fallacy is that a contract will protect a less than comprehensive specification – wrong!

Checklist

- Acquire a basic understanding of negotiation principles
- Encourage competition
- Negotiate everything – not just cost
- Never make assumptions
- Pay attention to Do's and Don'ts
- Use contracts depending on degree of risk
- Use model contracts where appropriate.

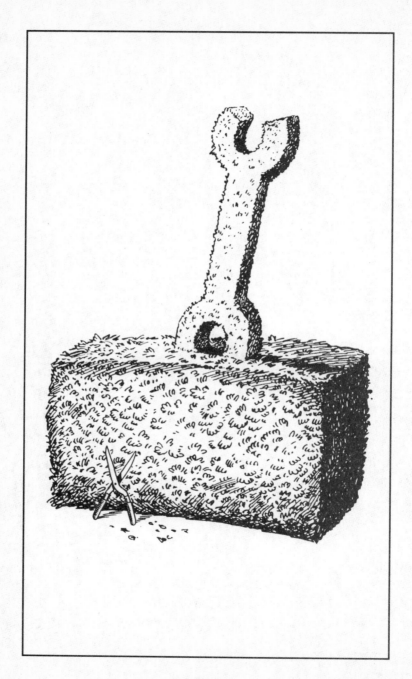

CHAPTER SEVEN

MAINTENANCE ─────────

Maintenance needs of buildings, plant and equipment vary according to the type and size of the organisation and the type of property occupied. There are numerous books written on this subject alone, including reference manuals and technical digests. This chapter attempts to cover some of the more universal issues associated with the management of maintenance and addresses:

- Centrally located premises
- Multiple location
- Engineering maintenance
- IT cabling

Also discussed options available on topics such as - standards, reactive and planned maintenance, cyclic maintenance, attic stocks, manuals, maintenance contracts and specifics including air-conditioning and lift maintenance.

Maintenance control

Maintenance is one area of a facilities manager's role which is often overlooked, or on occasions even ignored. It is however an area to which attention should be paid if the value of the initial investment in the building is to be maintained and a safe, healthy and efficient working environment is to be provided.

Maintenance costs can add a considerable amount to the operating costs of any company, and there will always be considerable pressures to reduce this area of expense. As this Chapter will explain, there are a number of ways that maintenance can be controlled to minimise waste and to maximise effectiveness.

Attention to detail, and obtaining competitively priced quotations for clearly defined maintenance needs is a better option than reducing maintenance costs by reducing services below certain minimum standards. To use the analogy of a motor car: a new car can be maintained or left unserviced. However a car that is maintained is more likely to start on a cold morning than one that isn't! The car owner suffers inconvenience but little else. However a building owner who through lack of maintenance loses the use of his building, also loses business and suffers financial loss.

Centrally located premises

A number of collocated office buildings, or a campus site, perhaps serving as a company's HQ can, in many ways, be thought of as one very large building. However, these buildings will probably vary in age, finishes, design and the degree of sophistication, requiring specific maintenance programmes for each.

The facilities manager's role is to establish maintenance standards for each building and maintain these standards within an agreed budget but how can this best be achieved?

Standards

Clearly the logical sequence would be to first agree standards, set a budget based on these requirements and follow a programme of preventative maintenance which would ensure standards are maintained. Unfortunately, all too often maintenance standards are driven by available funds and the facilities manager has to do the best he can within these cost parameters. However, whilst a subjective view can be taken in respect of many maintenance issues, such as how often to decorate the director's office, the facilities manager must stand his ground on health and safety related maintenance, or where a deferred job gives a short term saving but may create a more complex and costly problem in the future.

To document specific maintenance standards can be difficult however. For example how dirty do emulsin surfaces need to be before they are redecorated? It would be impracticable to formalise written standards. An alternative approach is to establish *minimum* requirements, based on essential health and safety works and the work needed to protect the asset value or your buildings. Available funds will then determine the extent of your maintenance schedules from here.

Maintenance classifications

Maintenance procedures fall into three main categories. You may see these referred to by other headings such as 'project maintenance' or 'regular maintenance' but for the purposes of clarity we will call them:

- Reactive maintenance
- Planned maintenance
- Cyclic maintenance checks

It is also important for the facilities manager to have a procedure for identifying works and this is best covered by cyclic maintenance checks.

Reactive maintenance

With reactive maintenance the facilities manager is, to some extent, dealing with the unknown. The requirement for maintenance may affect any part of the building, at any time and generally requires immediate action. Even here though, the facilities manager can plan and anticipate the need by identifying areas critical to the operation of a building and ensuring stocks of essential items are readily available. Similarly, suitable labour must be arranged to provide a 24 hour call out service as water pipes, for example, tend to burst at inconvenient times.

Planned maintenance

This covers maintenance items which are identified in sufficient time for them to be costed and programmed as separate 'mini' projects eg. redecoration of the main staircase or reception, replacement of solar control film to the windows. These items need not be actioned immediately which could have a negative impact on your budget figure, but can be brought forward to form part of next year's budget.

Alternatively, with the scale and critical status of the work identified, an informed decision can be made to exclude the work if dictated so by finances. However the facilities manager must ensure that any implications of exclusion are made clear to the person holding the 'purse strings' and that H&S issues are always dealt with.

Cyclic maintenance

Cyclic maintenance is work which is completed at predetermined periods, to specific areas, thereby changing the emphasis from reactive to proactive maintenance. Examples might be the regular treatment of special wood surfaces, clearing rainwater gutters and gullies, or servicing passenger lifts. All might cause serious problems if problems were allowed to develop before action was taken and for this reason an effective prompt system must be put in place.

Cyclic maintenance checks

The only way in which planned maintenance can work effectively is if an early warning system is in place to identify these items *before* they become critical. This is where cyclic maintenance checks can help.

Cyclic maintenance checks involve the regular *checking* of specified areas, to a predetermined programme. This process ensures that the facilities manager is kept in touch with the condition of his buildings and he/she can then prioritise work more effectively.

This checking process is the hub of an efficiently run maintenance facility as it necessitates the facilities manager, or his/her representative, inspecting all areas of each building, perhaps on a three monthly basis, depending on its age and design. This allows the facilities manager to identify:

- current or potential health and safety issues
- maintenance work before it is reported by the customer/user
- work required in the next budget period
- labour required for the next programming period
- materials needed which must be ordered prior to actioning the work

These building 'walkabouts' also have other less obvious advantages/opportunities which should be capitalised on by the facilities manager. These might include:

– Informal face to face feedback from users
– Inspection of other facilities, eg furniture, cleaning etc
– Checks on general housekeeping standards such as the orderly appearance of reception, cleanliness of waste bin areas
– Not least of all, being *seen* to care. Too often facilities managers become desk bound. Your customer will have more confidence in you understanding their concerns if they know you are in touch with the reality of the situation.
– Walk the building with your house manager or caretaker so that they are aware of the maintenance planned for the building and they can show you problems or areas of concern. This involvement can pay dividends in terms of user public relations, and enhances job satisfaction for the house manager.

Attic stock

The range and quantity of maintenance items you will need to hold in stock – usually known as attic stock – is dependant on a number of issues:

– manufacturers' and suppliers' leadtimes
– criticality of the item
– product continuity
– likelihood of batch differences
– availability of storage space
– storage costs
– susceptibility to damage while in store
– capital cost of items stored

Only you can assess the level of stock required, based on your own circumstances and measured against the above criteria. Remember however that whilst a degree of comfort can be had by holding every conceivable item you may require to maintain your building/s, there is a capital cost, storage charges (even if these are notional) and stock management.

Maintenance manuals

To aid the facilities manager and his team to carry out their duties each building should have its own maintenance manual. At its most detailed, a manual might include:

- Description of the building
- Emergency contacts
- Emergency equipment and procedures
- Contract consultants
- Authorities, consents and approvals
- Subcontractors and suppliers
- Maintenance contracts
- Floor loadings and restrictions
- General maintenance instructions
- Manufacturers' instruction leaflets index
- Fittings and component schedule index
- Services capacity, location and restrictions
- Services instructions
- Commissioning records and test certificates list
- Cleaning instructions
- Floor plans

To bring all this and, in some cases more, together in a single document or file appears a daunting task. However, by breaking it down into smaller parts and creating the framework and index for the file, information can be inserted as it becomes available during everyday maintenance of your building/s. Over a period you will build up a useful 'ready reference' for all maintenance issues.

A useful source of information is the architect who designed the building. Sometimes the production of a maintenance manual will form part of the construction contract and if you are a tenant you may find your landlord already has this information. If you are involved in the construction of a new building for your company's use you should give serious consideration to extending the architect's brief to include a manual, although this can be expensive.

The benefits will be the time saved in sourcing the correct item; warranties protected by the correct procedures being followed; and all information available to everyone and not held in a number of peoples' memories. In addition, your maintenance contractors will have a clear picture of how maintenance should be completed, and purchasing agreements can be set up *before* you need to buy anything.

Maintenance contracts

Carefully prepared contracts can be a life saver. When things are running smoothly a contract may not see the light of day. However, if service standards subside or hefty price increases are requested the contract should provide some means of redress. But beware ... a contract will be legally binding for both parties and payment terms, cost reviews and termination clauses are potential problem areas.

The contractor or supplier will often ask you to sign his standard contract, for the reasons outlined above but there will probably be a heavy bias in his favour. If you intend to sign a supplier contract *take advice* from a suitably qualified person. See Chapters 5 and 6.

Good maintenance contracts are not only useful in helping to resolve disputes or other problems, they also serve as a 'terms of reference' for the supplier. They stipulate exactly what is required of him and help to ensure a consistent service is provided throughout the duration of the contract.

The more your expenditure can be linked to well written contracts the less vulnerable you are.

Schedule of rates/day work

A schedule of rates is a list of unit prices for specific items of work, such as to supply and hang 1 sq m of wall covering. These rates can be agreed with a contractor by negotiation or competitive tender action.

If the contractor is likely to be asked to attend site frequently and carry out small quantities of work, his prices will reflect this and may be substantially higher than they would otherwise be for larger projects. For this reason the contractor should be given an indication of the likely scale and frequency, although this should not be contractually binding.

Whilst a schedule of rates offers the benefits of being able to cost out work quickly and relatively simply before an instruction to proceed is given, it can mean that more of your time is spent measuring, calculating and agreeing invoice costs with the contractor.

An alternative approach is to carry out tasks on day works where hourly rates or cost per day are agreed for each of the required trades. If this approach is used, it is better for a member of your own team to supervise the workforce. Supervision by the contractor over his own workforce offers no incentive for the contractor to complete the work swiftly - in fact on hourly rates, the converse is true. The benefits of this system are that it offers greater flexibility and makes it easier to action a number of small jobs without the need to measure the work.

As you will see, there are pros and cons for each approach and you must decide which system best fits your company's structure, type of work and required degree of control.

Materials selection

Selection of the correct materials must be considered *before* the item is needed and the proceeding advice on maintenance manuals refers to this.

The selection process should include the following:

- What did the architect use when the building was constructed and why was this selected?
- Required durability
- Ease of maintenance
- Leadtimes/availability
- Product continuity
- Alternatives
- Cost

Purchase cost savings can sometimes be a false economy if, for example, a door closure costing 10% less than your existing unit lasts for only half the time. The durability of an item can unfortunately only be fully tested in your installation. With items ranging from door closures to air conditioning plant, a PC database will help you to monitor in-use products and help with selection. Trends and potential problem areas can then be more easily identified for further investigation.

A final point on material selection is that new products are being brought to the market all the time and the facilities manager or his maintenance manager must keep abreast of new products and developments by reading the appropriate journals and visiting the occasional trade show.

Multiple locations

Despite the diversity and geographical spread of locations there are facilities management disciplines common to both centralised and multiple offices. The facilities to be provided to any location, whether it be Truro or Aberdeen, has to be uniform and to a high standard.

In essence it does not matter whether an office has 1,000 sq ft or 50,000 sq ft, the facilities provided to both are very similar, albeit that the scale of provision is different.

You will find that if multiple locations are left to arrange the various facilities for themselves, it usually results in different standards being accepted at each location. These standards can be either too high and unnecessary or usually, as in the majority of cases, too low, eg maintenance to buildings and equipment not carried out but exhibiting a spectacular floral display in reception.

Central control

Bringing maintenance under central control will give you the flexibility to use a number of methods to deal with the varied elements that make up maintenance.

The use of one or two contracts encompassing all the locations can give you the opportunity to obtain a much better outcome in contract negotiations than having to deal with a large number of individual local contracts. The use of a national contact with a detailed specification has worked well with a number of facilities as it allows you to set uniform standards right across the country in a single document. It will also ensure administration and accounting is made easier.

The detailed specification, with the following questions in mind, should set out in precise terms:

- What type of tasks are expected to be carried out?
- If planned, how frequent?
- What are the accepted standards going to be?
- What controls and supervision are required?
- What administrative service levels should be provided?
- What management information is needed?
- How are the operations going to be monitored?

This type of specification, linked with a good contract, will give you a basis for ensuring maintenance to a high standard.

Organisation

The benefits of a single contract dealing with a large number of multiple locations are many and varied.

Improved buying power obtained through negotiating centrally, a single point of contact with the contractor and much simpler administration all help in becoming more effective and efficient.

Being remote from the locations it is important to set up a point of contact with the contractor. Ideally, the contact should be as high as possible in the contractor's organisation. It is also beneficial to identify the contact's superior.

It is equally important that at each location there is a point of contact who will be able to co-ordinate information and instructions from the facilities manager and to be the contractor's local point of contact. The responsibilities placed at a local level are dependent on the amount of administrative autonomy you wish to delegate.

Guidelines

To have every maintenance query channelled through head office can be time consuming and perhaps lead to a resourcing burden. On the other hand to allow the multiple locations to have complete control could create a cost control problem. A solution to this problem would be to provide guidelines to the locations.

Guidelines should meet the needs of both Head Office and nationwide locations to ensure a high quality office environment without being extravagant. The great advantage of guidelines are that they can be controlled centrally and easily.

The guidelines can set out specifically those types of maintenance items which can be carried out without referral to the facilities manager. These are usually minor items of repair or renewal and cover the full range of day-to-day maintenance items. It is also a good idea to fix a monetary limit for these repairs or renewals to ensure no larger maintenance items are carried out without prior approval. A nominal figure of £50 to £100 can be set depending on the amount of work to be dealt with centrally.

There is an education process required to be implemented with the locations point of contact to ensure that maintenance call-outs are cost effective, eg that three or four items of work arise before a maintenance visit is required. This aspect can be addressed in your guidelines.

Contractors' register

At each location a maintenance contractors response register should be available, giving details of:

- Date and time the contractor was contacted.
- A brief description of the work to be carried out.
- Date and time the contractor arrived.
- Any additional work carried out.
- Date and time work completed.
- Contractor's signature.

The register can be sent from the locations on a regular basis or faxed if a particular query arises. It is useful to have the register available to check against the contractors work sheets and invoices.

The register has another useful purpose in that recurring maintenance items can be identified easily and rectified by a more permanent arrangement by absorbing the work within a planned programme of maintenance.

Authorisation

Should the contractor arrive on site and find that the estimated amount of work required by the location is in excess of the fixed monetary limit the contractor has to request authorisation from the facilities manager, who gives verbal clearance *or* requests a written quotation to be submitted prior to any work being started. It is convenient for administration purposes to have a different prefix for order numbers that emanate from central facilities management.

Any work that is deemed to be of a health and safety nature or an emergency repair is normally accepted as a priority with no monetary limit, however it is important that control of the work is passed from the location to the facilities manager as soon as possible to ensure that only necessary work is being carried out.

Invoices

With only one or two main contractors carrying out work the opportunities are available to set in place an administrative invoice system that is most suitable.

To help meet the criteria suggested in the chapter dealing with cost control, the checking and approval of invoices could be processed using a summary sheet with individual invoices attached. This sheet should give details on:

- location
- where the work was carried out
- invoice number

- value
- your accounting reference

This format does not have to be printed, as most large contractors have computers that use compatible software and therefore the information can be held on a disc, which can be sent, approved and payment made under the payment terms.

General

One final point is the remoteness of a location should not mean that good maintenance practices are not carried out. The process has been covered earlier in the chapter and should ensure a good standard of maintenance at multiple locations.

Engineering Maintenance

So far, this chapter has dealt with the more general issues of building maintenance. The engineering systems within modern buildings do, however, have additional maintenance requirements over and above those or routine maintenance. The principal reasons for maintaining engineering plant and equipment are:

- Ensuring satisfactory working conditions for staff
- Increased reliability of plant
- Increased energy efficiency of equipment
- Environmental compliance

Consequently engineering related maintenance costs can, to a greater or lesser degree, be considered to have an element of 'payback', ie money not spent on maintenance can be "lost" through operating inefficiencies of plant and equipment.

Principal aspects

A maintenance and inspection schedule indicates typical tasks and frequencies which require to be carried out in an air conditioned accommodation under a planned maintenance regime. Each piece of plant and equipment will have its own specific maintenance needs, details of which can be obtained from the original manufacture for large, complex items or by applying common sense for smaller simpler items ie a check on pipework and valves would entail visually checking for leaks, rusting, damage etc.

Maintenance tasks can be broken down into a number of generic headings. These can generally be summarised as:

● Air conditioning maintenance
● Mechanical services maintenance
● Electrical services maintenance
● Lifts maintenance

Looking at each of these headings in turn, the need for maintenance is as follows:

Air conditioning

The plant and equipment required to be maintained are:

– *Air handling plant* : to ensure that the conditioned air is delivered to the spaces where it is required. Maintenance will need to include motor/fan pulleys and belts; humidifiers and associated water treatment and hygiene systems (if installed); changing of filters etc.
– *Chillers* : to ensure that the necessary cooling is available to provide cool air from the air handling plant.

113

Maintenance will need to include for checking refrigerant and oil levels; system pressures and current draws; operation of safety controls etc.

– *Controls* : to ensure that the air conditioning system works when required, in the manner required whilst at the same time ensuring that the system is operating efficiently. Maintenance would typically include: calibration of sensors; checking of control set points; time clock settings; operation of plant inter-locks etc.

– *Ductwork/air distribution systems* : to ensure that the conditioned air is being delivered (and extracted) from all areas of the building as originally designed. Maintenance will need to include for: the correct setting of all balancing dampers, the operation of all fire and smoke dampers (of both the fusible link and motorised types) and the cleanliness of ductwork with particular attention paid to any bacteriological infection of the ductwork/air distribution systems.

Mechanical services

The plant and equipment requiring maintenance under this heading can be briefly described as:

– *Boilers* (including burners) : to ensure that heating and hot water is generated when required and at maximum efficiency. Maintenance will need to check: correct operation of boiler safety temperature controls; the condition and cleanliness of the boiler flue ways to ensure maximum heat transfer can occur; the correct air/fuel ratios at the burner to ensure maximum operating efficiencies.

– *Pumps* : to ensure that the heating and hot water is circulated around the building to those areas where it is needed. Maintenance will need to include: pulley belts and bearings are all in good condition; that any auto-changeover switches work when a pump fails.

– *Hot and cold water storage systems* : to ensure that the hot and cold water systems store and distribute water at the correct temperatures and in a fit and safe condition to be used. Maintenance will need to include: checking and recording of storage and distribution water temperatures to comply with H & S Document HS(G)70; periodic cleaning of systems to ensure that sediment and other potential sources which could harbour bacteria do not exist; checking and calibration of controls on hot water cylinders to ensure that water temperatures do not exceed a safe temperature above which people could be scalded.

Electrical services

The plant and equipment requiring maintenance under this heading can be briefly described as:

- *Fixed electrical systems* : to ensure that the electrical installation within the building is in a safe and fit condition. Alterations to existing systems should be strictly controlled and should under no circumstances be carried out by unqualified personnel. Maintenance requirements should include: regular visual inspections of installation to ensure that no exposed cables/conductors exist and that the installation has not suffered any physical damage. Apart from ensuring that the installation is covered by a valid testing certificate (which is usually valid for five years) regular testing of safety devices - ie residual current devices (RCD's) should also be undertaken.
- *Portable appliances* : to ensure the portable appliances, which are the greatest potential source of electrical shock or fire, are safe and fit for use. Maintenance requirements include checking that plugs are correctly wired, contain the correct fuse and that the appliance is adequately earthed. It is generally considered that annual testing is appropriate for portable appliances, although this frequency should be increased where it is likely that abuse of appliances may occur, eg in a workshop.

- *Emergency lighting* : to ensure that all emergency light and internally illuminated exit signs will work when required. Maintenance should include: routine discharge testing to ensure that the support batteries can maintain the emergency lighting for the required duration as required by the appropriate British Standard; checking to see that all escape routes are covered by emergency lights and that no new routes have been created, particularly in open plan offices, which may not be illuminated.
- *Fire alarm systems* : to ensure that the system fully functions in the event of activation, and that all alarm points, (both manual and automatic), sounders and associated devices work correctly. This will include automatic door releases, smoke dampers etc. Maintenance will need to include the routine testing and activation of *all* devices, as well as checking the condition of charges, transformers, back-up batteries etc. Audibility checks will also need to be included particularly if large numbers of offices are periodically built and demolished within existing open plan floors.

Lifts

To be safe and reliable, lifts and other forms of mechanical travel ie hoists, escalators etc will require regular maintenance and inspection. Although this is very much a specialist maintenance item, it is necessary to ensure that 'car' safety controls are kept in working order, that lift ropes are not frayed and that the lift controls are reliable. Lifts generally suffer damage from irate staff 'thumping' call buttons because the lift either doesn't arrive when called or due to annunciator lights not indicating where the lift is located.

Records

In all the maintenance activities, it is important to maintain good, clear and informative records. These will enable the facilities manager to be able to judge whether the maintenance is cost effective, whether it is resulting in reduced breakdowns, and most importantly enable the manager to demonstrate that the plant and equipment were maintained in a safe operating condition as required by the Health & Safety Executive.

Staff

Finally, as with any form of maintenance, the work can be carried out on an 'in-house' basis, using directly employed staff, or by contracting part or all of the work to one of the numerous maintenance companies in the market place. Your decision will probably be based on economics and company policy. There is no right or wrong answer to this, the best solution is the one which provides most benefit to your organisation.

Considerations within buildings for IT cabling

This section covers the issues associated with a successful information technology (IT) cabling installation.

One definition of a successful cabling installation is one which meets todays business needs, in the most cost effective way, while also providing a means of supporting future requirements.

Information technology (IT) cabling

IT cabling is the cabling used to communicate information between two locations. It is commonly described in terms of the applications supported. Typical examples are:

- telephone
- data
- personal computers/LANs
- printing

- image/video
- Control and telemetry signals
- Specialist applications such as computer suite or communications room cabling

Choice of cabling

Cabling type will often differ depending upon the application or equipment supported, the requirements for physical and electromagnetic protection, transmission performance, resilience to failure etc.
Examples of common cable types include:

- unshielded twisted pair (UTP)
- shielded twisted pair (STP)
- fibre optic
- coax/twinax
- multicore

Each one is available in a variety of grades and sizes. The selection of the appropriate specification cable involves consideration of all current and future needs, physical space within cableways, and the requirements of the various regulatory bodies, the equipment/service providers and maintainer.

Cabling schemes

Cabling installation within a building may be described as ad-hoc or structured.

Ad-hoc

Here, cables are installed only as needed for immediate use. The advantages of this approach are mainly short term. They are:

- Minimum initial installation costs
- Reduced riser and cable way congestion.

The potential disadvantages include:

- The need to relocate or install additional cables each time an office area is changed
- Higher unit costs when relocating existing or installing additional connections
- Disruption to furniture and partitions to gain access to cableways
- Difficulty and delays in providing connections to the required location
- Difficulty in maintaining detailed cabling records.

Structured

The principle of a structured cabling scheme is to 'saturate' an area (for instance, a floor) with pre-wired outlets. The method of cabling is uniform and logical, and provides connectivity for a large number of current and future applications, all with just one or two cable runs to each user station/desk.

The advantages include:

- Relocation of equipment can often be completed within minutes
- Minimal disruption to staff while undertaking changes
- Fixed unit costs to undertake a change
- Future connection needs catered for

The disadvantages include:

- High initial capital outlay
- Overall utilisation of the installed cabling is low

Cableways

Typically, IT cable runs are from the street (in the case of public telecommunications operator (PTO) landline services) and/or the roof (for microwave and satellite services) through risers and ducts to equipment rooms, and then on through raised floors or suspended ceilings to the required end User station/desks.

119

All these routes need to have suitable trunking, trays or conduits to contain and separate the necessary cables. Care needs to be taken to ensure that, in particular, cableways for the likes of BT and Mercury (PTO) services are clearly identified and have adequate capacity for future growth.

All technical, fire and planning regulations should be adhered to. It is also necessary to consider the need for:

- Separate PTO and internal cable distribution schemes
- Segregation of IT and power cabling
- Adequate earth bonding points
- Maintaining the integrity of fire breaks
- Suitable fixing points for overhead catenary suspension wires
- Cable insulation with low smoke properties (plenum cable)
- Movement of installed cabling when relocating end user connection points within, for instance, a floor trap

Equipment room specifications

When considering accommodation for computer and communication equipment rooms it may be necessary to consider:

- Reinforcement for walls for cable frames or wall mounted equipment
- Layout of the equipment within the room, providing space for maintenance access
- Health and safety, and regulatory requirements
- Cable entry and exit points
- Power requirements for each item of equipment, including the need for 'clean' earth bonding and uninterruptible power supplies (UPS)
- Temperature and humidity monitoring and control
- Ventilation (particularly if wet cell batteries are to be used for standby power)
- Fire alarm and extinguishing methods
- Access security and control
- Provision for future growth

Outlet connection points

Cable connection points may be mounted within floor traps, from ceiling feeds, and on wall or partition surfaces. The appropriate choice will depend on the following factors:

- Expected rate of movement of partitions, desks etc
- 'Geography' of the accommodation
- Type of cable and cabling scheme to be installed
- Expected rate of office changes

Future proofing

In order to ensure that the cabling installation will cater for future changes it is necessary to consider:

- Staff growth
- Office moves
- Introduction of new/different technology; for instance PCs or workstations
- Skill required to implement changes

For each of the above changes it is likely that the installed cabling will need to be changed or adapted to cater for the new requirement. With sufficient thought at the time of cabling installation it will be possible to readily undertake such changes in a cost effective way.

Checklist

- Centrally located premises
- Specify your standards

- Classify your maintenance categories:
    Reactive
    Planned
    Cyclic
- Identify cyclic checks
- Consider requirements for attic stock
- Prepare maintenance manuals for each building
- Set up maintenance contracts
- Agree schedule of rates in advance
- Take care with materials selection

● Multiple locations

- Set up your systems for central control
- Identify responsibilities within your organisation
- Prepare guidelines for routine maintenance
- Draw up a contractors' register
- Publish authorisation limits
- Define checklists for invoice approval
- Remote locations should not affect your standards

● Engineering maintenance

- Define the principal aspects of your maintenance programme
- Consider special requirements for
    Air conditioning
    Mechanical services
    Electrical services
    Lifts
- Records will help you to monitor the effectiveness of your servicing programme
- Agree your policy for using in-house or contracted staff

● IT Cabling

- Consider different options available
- Decide on ad-hoc or structured cabling schemes
- Identify cable ways and trunking methods
- Your equipment rooms will need special consideration
- Identify which outlets best suit your installation
- Consider your future needs

CHAPTER EIGHT

ENERGY MANAGEMENT —————

One of the largest areas of expenditure facing most facilities managers will be that of energy. It may also prove to be the most difficult upon which to make a major impact. Reducing energy consumption will result in reduced energy costs. However, this Chapter will attempt to demonstrate an understanding of the processes that result in energy usage, and implementation of the correct energy and cost saving techniques can result in substantially higher savings than those achieved by simply turning something off.

This chapter will therefore deal with:

- Monitoring and targeting of energy usage.
- Energy sources, choices and tariffs.
- Opportunities and vulnerabilities in energy and cost savings.
- Energy saving initiatives.

Monitoring and targeting: Measuring efficiency

One of the fundamental elements of any management system is that of measuring the efficiency of the process in question. This holds goods for a variety of processes from one of pure production on an assembly line through to the creative processes involved in a design team.

The way in which a building uses energy can be compared to how the human metabolism expends energy to regulate the body's internal environment. The two main considerations as to whether we perspire or shiver are:

- The type of work and the rate at which we are working.
- The environment around us.

Similarly for a building, the requirement to heat and cool it will depend on the nature and amount of work being carried out on its floors and the weather outside it. Energy used by catering, hot water and lighting requirements will also be a factor. So, the problem you face in trying to manage the energy that your building consumes is how to:

- Determine what influences the buildings energy use.
- Measure the energy used against these factors.
- Set targets for improving how much energy is used compared to these influencing factors.

Or, to put this simply, you need to use monitoring and targeting.

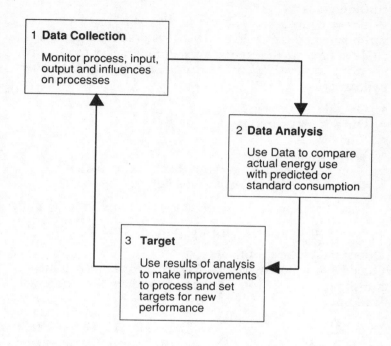

(Figure 8.1)

The concept of energy – 'centres' and energy 'drivers'

Anything that uses energy is an energy 'centre', anything that influences how much that centre uses is an energy 'driver'.

Typically the main energy users or energy centres in an office building are air-conditioning, lighting, heating, small power (socket outlets for personal computers etc), hot water services and catering (if any facilities exist in the building). Obviously, if there is some special process being

127

undertaken inside the buildings, this may need to be considered as well.

These centres may be further broken down into the various main components of each system, boilers, pumps, chillers, fans etc. Energy drivers although easy to identify, are not always so easy to measure. Consider the following typical 'drivers':

- Outside air temperature
- Outside air humidity
- Sunshine
- Windspeed
- Occupancy periods and numbers of occupancy
- Control settings (thermostats etc).

Some of these are easy to measure, others are not.

Now consider these 'drivers' in more detail:

Outside air temperature ⎫
Outside air humidity ⎬ Variable drivers which influence
Sunshine ⎪ heating and air conditioning
Windspeed ⎭

Occupancy ⎫ Drivers which may be considered
Control Settings ⎬ 'constant' which affect all energy
⎭ centres

If we consider the 'constant' drivers to be truly constant then measurement is simplified. The variable or weather related drivers are now considered.

Degree days

Degree days are a widely accepted method of assessing the driver of outside air temperature.

If we consider the analogy of the human body once more, there are times when we are at 'equilibrium' with our rate of work and the environment around us. That is we are 'free wheeling', requiring no perspiring or shivering, energy being burned up purely for the work in hand and maintaining our functional processes.

Once again this can be applied to a building, there will be certain periods of the year when a building is in balance with its environment and no heating or cooling is required. When considering the heating of a building the following equation indicates what is happening at any one time:

Heat input required = Heat lost through building envelope (glass, walls, floors, ceilings etc)

Plus + Heat lost to air flowing through building from outside (ventilation and 'infiltration')

Less - Heat given off into space by people

Less - Heat given off into space by machines and lighting

Less - Heat into space from sunshine.

During winter the strength and duration of sunshine or 'solar gain' into a building is usually minimal and therefore ignored. However, people, machines and lights will contribute a considerable amount of heat to an office building during the heating season, so some allowance needs to be made.

If we were to ignore this, then the heating required for a building to maintain an internal air temperature of say 21°C, would be directly proportional to the difference between 21°C and the outside air temperature. However, due to the effect of heat gains from people, lights and machines, in practice, heating is not required until the outside temperature drops well below 21°C. Some other 'base' temperature needs to be used. The most common one being 15.5°C (which is the base for published degree day data). This model is used in calculating theoretical energy usage.

Unfortunately, although very useful, this model is crude since the weather is very unpredictable. Nevertheless, methods using degree days should not be rejected outright. There are some particularly useful techniques, especially those related to monitoring the performance of heating systems in terms of energy use. One such method is introduced later in this Chapter (the normalised performance indicator).

For a fuller description of degree days and their use refer to: The Chartered Institute of Engineers' (CIBSE) Guide, Volume A, 1986; Fuel Efficiency Booklet No 7, 'Degree Days', published by the Energy Efficiency Office, 1987.

The problems with air-conditioning

So, the story so far is that we can:

- Breakdown the building's energy centres and monitor the energy use of each.
- Consider the building's energy drivers as 'constant' and 'variable'.
- Measure the constant drivers.
- Attempt to measure the variable driver of outside air temperature by using degree days.
- Use comparisons of energy centres to energy drivers in order to monitor energy performance and project energy targets.

The problems that energy managers will face with buildings is how to measure the energy drivers influencing air conditioning. During the 'cooling season', sunshine or 'solar gain' is an important factor as is outside air humidity and of course temperature. It should be remembered that in terms of energy cost, it usually costs more to air condition a building than it does to heat it. So if possible it makes sense to treat this individually.

External air humidity and temperature can be measured and their influences assessed, since as for heating the relationship between cooling load to these drivers may be considered linear over the season. However, the way in which solar gain affects a building is extremely complex. The influence of sunshine is modified by:

- Ratio of glazing to wall/roof area and floor plan area.
- Type of glass and internal or external shading;
- Ratio of potential solar load against other loads 'driving' the air conditioning (eg for a computer centre or trading floor, the element of solar gain, compared to the heat given off by the computers or people, will be very small);

Unfortunately, due to the presence of the solar gain driver, it is not reasonably possible to be totally sure of the monitoring and targeting figures for air conditioning systems. However, this is no reason for not using such a system. Provided that the manager is aware of the possible influence of the solar driver, it will still be possible to achieve very useful and repeatable results within a band of tolerance.

Establishing monitoring & targeting

The start of any monitoring and targeting (M & T) system will involve establishing an energy audit of the building or buildings concerned. In its simplest form, this will entail collating data available from the energy bills. For a more rigorous M&T system, this audit should break down this data and log the energy used by each energy centre.

Working with basic data, a simple M&T performance monitor has been developed by the Energy Efficiency Office (DoE). They have used statistical building data to formulate the concept of a 'normalised performance indicator' (NPI). This attempts to provide some allowance for the effect of weather on building energy use, by considering degree days (heating degree days not cooling). This has resulted in the publication of performance yardsticks for typical buildings, in terms of kilowatt hours per square metre of floorspace per year (kWh/m^2 year).

For reasons already discussed the tolerance on these bands is fairly wide. However, they are a very useful tool for energy managers establishing an M&T system. By using the NPI method a manager can quickly see how different buildings are performing. It is also a good idea to produce a league table if operating more than one building and produce trends if historical billing data is available.

True monitoring and targeting should go further than this if large buildings or complexes of buildings are under scrutiny.

More accurate information on the energy drivers and energy centres needs to be sought. The amount of data being handled usually means that the use of a personal computer is viable. Furthermore, many modern buildings are equipped with computerised building management systems (BMS), especially if they are fully air conditioned. BMS can provide extremely useful data on both energy centres and drivers.

Some other useful reading on the subject of M&T and energy audits is produced by the DoE and CIBSE respectively. However, it is recommended that those managers who are not engineering biased, seek assistance and advice from suitably qualified and experienced energy professionals.

It should also be borne in mind that the whole point of M&T is to monitor performance and set subsequent targets for improving performance – ie save energy! There is no point in setting targets that cannot be met and it is here that an engineering professional is needed to carefully evaluate proposals for energy savings.

Some potential areas for saving energy and the ways in which these should be assessed are discussed later in this Chapter under 'Energy saving initiatives'.

Source choices and tariffs

Theoretically, building owners and operators can choose from a wide range of fuels. These can include not only conventional fuels such as electricity, gas, oil and coal but also the more unusual ones of solar power, chp (combined heat and power), geothermal, waste gas reclamation etc. However most facilities managers will find that their choices are relatively limited, particularly if they are located in town or city centres.

Assuming availability, and that the type of energy is appropriate to your needs, details of various fuels can be described as follows:

Electricity

The most widely used source of energy is likely to be electricity although the percentage it forms of any company's total energy bill will vary depending upon its usage, ie lighting, heating, manufacturing process etc. You will therefore invariably be faced with the choice of a number of tariffs and electricity suppliers, the suitability of which will be dependant upon a number of factors. These factors would include such things as hours of usage, peak usage (maximum demand), load profile etc.

Where the maximum demand is less than 1 megawatt (1MW) then you will be limited to the published tariffs on offer from the local supply company. The address of the local company can be obtained from the telephone directory.

Generally each area supplier will be able to offer a number of tariffs to suit a range of options. These ranges will generally cover usage levels up to 50 KVA maximum demand, and usage levels above this figure. These ranges will be available at daytime (24 hour) rates and off-peak rates (reduced charges for night time usage). For the above 50 KVA consumer, 'time-of-day' tariffs are applicable, where the unit cost of electricity is charged at various costs throughout the day.

In simple terms the category in which you are likely to find your building will be as follows:

1 Less than 50 KVA : small shop, suite of offices, small factory unit

2 Greater than 50 KVA (daytime usage) : medium/large shop, self-contained offices, manufacturing factory unit

3 Greater than 50 KVA (off-peak rates) : as 2 above but where a known night time usage of electricity occurs

4 'time of day' tariffs : as 2 above but where the user has the capability of either substantially reducing load/usage during 'penalty' periods, or where alternative sources of supply (ie generators) are available.

The local supply company will invariably advise on the selection of the correct tariff to suit the customers' needs. Where large numbers of premises are involved, covering a number of the supply areas, then the use of utility analyst companies can be cost effective. These companies will analyse electricity usage, compare the cost benefits of the various tariffs and recommend charges of tariff where appropriate. Their costs are generally covered by a share of any savings achieved.

Following the privatisation of the electricity supply industry in 1989, consumers having a maximum demand in excess of 1000 KVA (1 MVA) became able to negotiate with suppliers outside of their geographical location. (From 1994 this figure will reduce enabling many more medium sized building operators to shop around for better deals).

To obtain the most beneficial rates you will need to be able to demonstrate to any supplier certain information about your load, ie maximum demand (MD), daily load profile, seasonal variances etc. The greater the demand at peak periods the less attractive the load to any supplier.

Help in establishing load profiles can be obtained from either the existing supply authority or from any responsible energy management company. In the latter case a fee would be chargeable dependent upon the work involved.

Gas

Unless the core business of your company is manufacturing where gas is used in the main manufacturing process, or where space heating forms the major energy usage, ie in a factory or warehouse, then gas costs are likely to be only equal to or generally less than electricity costs.

Despite privatisation, British Gas is likely to remain the sole supply option available to most facility managers for some time. Although British Gas does have a tariff structure, the levels of consumption necessary to qualify are quite large. The tariff structure consists of a number of increasing consumption bands with a corresponding decrease in cost bands.

Consumption levels below 25,000 therms will generally not be covered by any special tariffs and normally standard rate charges apply. Consequently, facilities managers responsible for one or two buildings will currently find little scope for manoeuvre, but where an organisation has a number of buildings the consumptions can be amalgamated to move into more beneficial rate bands.

Although competition is starting to appear in the gas supply market place, it is unlikely that small scale users will find any great benefit. However this may change as additional alternative suppliers enter the market place.

Oil

The use of oil will invariably be limited to use as a heating fuel, except where it is used as the fuel source for either permanent or emergency power generation or as the primary fuel in manufacturing processes eg steam generators.

Fuel oil can be obtained in a number of forms, generally determined by its viscosity. It ranges from light fuel oil through to heavy fuel oil. Each grade of oil will have its own particular storage and distribution requirements, which prevents the fuels from being readily interchanged. The oil burning equipment will also be specifically matched against a particular type of oil.

The burning of oil, particularly the heavy grades being a sulphur bearing fuel, is affected by the Clean Air Act and any changes of plant should be referred to the local authority.

Oil can be obtained from a number of suppliers, both local and national, and charges will vary considerably depending upon type of oil the location of the site and the quantity required. As oil incurs delivery charges, it is more economical to take full tanker deliveries if possible to minimise these charges. It is however worthwhile shopping around and avoiding long term contracts as suppliers rates will vary from time to time.

Coal

It is likely that you will be faced with the choice of using coal. Like oil, it is a sulphur bearing fuel and the products of its combustion are covered by the Clean Air Act. It also has storage and distribution problems not associated with the 'clean' fuels of gas or electricity.

Opportunities and vulnerabilities

Depending upon the size of your organisation, the type of operation undertaken, and the type of premises, other opportunities and even vulnerabilities can have an effect on energy usage and costs. Although not all of the following will be applicable to most facilities managers a broad understanding of these opportunities and vulnerabilities may prove useful. These are:

- CHP (combined heat and power) and private generation.
- Interruptible fuel arrangements
- Competence of site personnel
- Contract energy management

CHP and private generation

Although CHP (combined heat and power) and private generation are loosely related, since they both entail generation of electricity, the reasons for their selection will be entirely different.

Combined heat and power systems will only be economic, as the name suggests, where there are requirements for both heat and electrical consumption. In a CHP system the 'waste' heat from the electricity generation process is reclaimed and used. In situations where the need for waste heat is intermittent, eg in central heating systems, then the economics of CHP may not prove cost effective. However, where a process requiring heat on a continuous basis exists together with a 'matched' electrical requirement, then the economics of a CHP system come into their own.

Private generation is unlikely to be economic except to the extremely large user or where interruptible tariffs create an economic case. The inefficiencies of electrical generation coupled to fuel prices will result in this not being viable for most facilities managers.

However, where electricity can be generated using either 'free' fuel, for example methane gas from land fill sites, or where waste energy from a manufacturing process is available to power turbines, then private generation can become economic. It is worth noting that privately generated electricity can be 'exported', that is to say fed back into the grid and sold to the regional electricity supply company.

Interruptible fuel arrangements

As the name suggests, this option is based on the right of the supply company, which can be either electrical or gas, to interrupt the supply of power for extended periods at relatively short notice. Because this means that the supply companies can control their peak loads without having to buy at peak prices, they offer preferential rates to those consumers who are prepared to switch to alternative power sources.

Typically this would mean generating your own electricity during periods of supply interruption, switching to an alternative fuel. As with most of these options they are unlikely to be cost effective to the small energy user as the capital costs involved in installing generator or dual fuel burners is likely to considerably outstrip any short term energy savings and will result in extended payback periods.

Competence of site personnel

Although modern plant runs automatically, it still requires to be operated correctly. It is therefore necessary that the personnel responsible for energy have a broad understanding of the process, where the plant and controls are and how they operate.

Plant and equipment which is poorly maintained will inevitably be more expensive to run; plant and equipment which is left running when it is not required wastes energy whilst plant and equipment which is no longer appropriate to the need, eg specialist extract plant for a process which has been discontinued, will consume energy unnecessarily.

It is therefore important that the person tasked with managing energy or the person or company responsible for maintaining the plant and equipment are competent to do so. It is probable that, in most cases, greater savings can be achieved by operating plant and equipment properly and efficiently than by any other means.

Contract energy management

A large number of companies, particularly if they are not in manufacturing, will probably not have staff employed just to deal with energy nor with the experience to fully develop the role. Consequently a number of companies have entered the market place to fill this void.

These companies will usually offer a package whereby they manage the energy costs and undertake the plant and equipment maintenance for an agreed fee. In some cases they will also undertake to replace faulty plant and equipment within their contract. In many cases these agreements can be beneficial in that with a fixed fee agreement you are at least able to know that a potential area of variable cost is strictly controlled. However, you should compare the true cost of the services provided with the energy expenditure that could be expected by the introduction of a simple monitoring and targeting system and by the use of competent maintenance personnel.

Some of the less reputable contract energy management companies have in the past attracted a reputation for achieving their profit at the expense of the maintained conditions. By turning the heating thermostat down by 1°C can result in a reduced heating bill of 5-10%. Consequently a clear agreement setting out conditions to be maintained, hours of opening etc should be established with any contract energy company you might consider employing.

Energy-saving initiatives

There are, it seems, a myriad of wonderful 'do it all' energy-saving gadgets on the market. The unsuspecting facilities manager may be forgiven for feeling the pressure to invest and 'save energy'.

However some thoughts should be foremost when considering energy saving.

The best options are designed in at the outset of any building project

Many of these aspects may be passive – ie part of the building fabric itself, such as external shading, natural ventilation, good use of daylight etc.

Cost saving is not always the same as energy saving

For example, the practice of making ice at night in an ice storage air conditioning system usually results in greater energy use. However the energy cost is reduced by 'peak lopping' and use of off peak electrical tariff.

When considering payback look at the overall picture, don't wear blinkers

For example, when installing a heat recovery heat exchanger into an air system, extra resistance to air flow will result in more fan power being required for the same volume of air moved. The extra electrical consumption should be deducted from the heat energy recovered. Also, don't overlook additional maintenance costs (cleaning etc).

Start with good housekeeping

There is little point in investing in extra equipment if the manager has no idea of which area or even which building is most inefficient. It may be possible to make considerable savings without capital investment, simply by checking that everything is 'in order'. Perhaps the best start is an energy audit then to progress to monitoring and targeting (see earlier section).

Good housekeeping – closing the loop

One of the fundamentals of 'good housekeeping' is that of planned maintenance. This has been discussed earlier, however two important aspects with respect to energy are:

- Maximising plant running efficiency
- Providing useful data on control settings etc and ensuring that these are not unduly 'tampered with'.

Having run an energy audit and initiated a basic M&T system there may be good reason to consider a design review. Buildings and the systems are designed to a mutual brief between the client and the professional team (architect, engineers etc). Usually a specification is then produced by the team, which is interpreted by the contractors who actually build the project.

The various contractural problems along this 'chain' are well documented. The fundamental problems arise whenever misinterpretation occurs between what is envisaged by one party and what is perceived by another.

Couple this with the fact that many of the 'clients' are not the building end user and the argument for a design review is convincing.

The idea of a design review is to 'close the loop' and provide feedback information to correct misfits between the original concept, design and specification, installation as installed and installation as actually used by occupant. In many instances it may be possible to re-commission the building systems and control set points to suit how the building is *actually* being used. Don't forget that a building may not remain static for long due to the space planning requirements and property strategy of the occupying company.

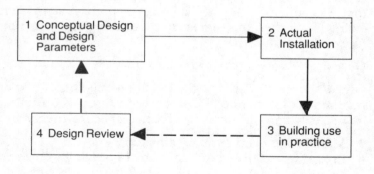

'Closing the loop'
(Figure 8.2)

Typical methods for saving energy in offices

As already stated, the number of energy-saving devices is so great that a book could be produced on these alone. There is not scope within this text to go into technical detail. Nevertheless as a 'taster' to those uninitiated in this subject here are a few more common ideas:

'Passive' or 'built in' methods

Good use of insulation – reduces heat loss from building and engineering systems. In the latter case this ensures that heat transfers occur when they are supposed to and not along the distribution routes.
– Good use of daylight – roof lights, correct window to room dimension ratios etc.
– Internal or external solar shading
– Natural ventilation wherever possible
– Low emissivity glazing

Mechanical/electrical systems

Combined heat and power (CHP) – private generation of electricity (diesel or gas fired reciprocating engines) coupled with heat recovery from the generating sets. If the heat can be usefully recovered and used for example, to heat a swimming pool, the electricity generated becomes economical.

Great care needs to be taken to ensure that CHP is viable for the building considered. However, there are many successful examples of these installations.

Thermal storage. A building's heating or cooling load will vary considerably throughout a 24 hour period. In a basic system, the cooling and heating plant will be sized to meet the 'peak' or greatest demand. This results in large plant and equipment which for most of the day (and in fact most of the year since 'design' days rarely occur), running at part load and inefficiency.

The thermal store is utilised to create a buffer of heat or cooling capacity. The store is charged during the 'off peak' hours when the building is unoccupied and used to 'top up' the cooling or heating plant during the occupied period. In this way the cooling and heating plant is able to be sized smaller but allowed to run for longer at full load.

Use may be made of off peak electricity, power cable or gas main sizing to heating and cooling plant is smaller etc. Care must be taken when analysing the 'pay back' period of such installations, the costs of the thermal store and the possible associated structural requirements needs to be offset against the predicted savings.

Skill is also required when selecting the store and heating/ cooling plant options. The sizing of one depends on the other.

Heat exchangers. Various types may often be considered to recover heat from waste air in order to preheat fresh air entering the building. These may be appropriate in air conditioning systems. The costs of maintenance and the extra fan power required to overcome the resistance of the heat exchanger to air flow need consideration.

Solar collectors. Since their advent, little impact has been made into the building services sector by solar cells and solar collectors. The high capital costs involved, the low grade of energy obtained and the periods this energy is available, rarely make solar power a viable commercial option in Britain.

One area that may be worth considering though, is the use of solar powered external lighting.

Building management systems and control. There is no doubt that close control of temperature and time settings etc also optimises the building's energy use. Large installations may often benefit from the addition of a computerised management systems.

Very often retrofit of controls will bring fast payback on older systems where existing control is not close and as a result energy is wasted.

All too often though, controls are installed and then forgotten about. They should be inspected, cleaned and calibrated etc on a regular basis. To get the most of a BMS installation, in house or contracted expertise should be in attendance to monitor and make adjustments as necessary.

Lighting control. Office lighting is a major power consumer. There are many forms of controlling the switching of lighting including occupancy detectors, daylight detection through to computer (BMS) control to dim lights at strategic periods of the day.

Usually these options are best 'designed in'. In retrofit situations costly circuiting of the electrical wiring is often required to arrange for rational switching of the lighting. However, for large installations there may still be viable pay-back.

Energy efficient lighting. Undoubtedly the most efficient light is daylight! However low power lamps and high frequency lighting with improved automatic dimming facilities are often good options.

Estimating payback

Unfortunately, the amount of energy recovered from a system or energy saving device will very often be weather dependant. For example, consider the case of a heat exchanger installed into an air conditioning system, which uses the extract air temperature to pre-heat incoming fresh air in winter. The energy transferred to the fresh air is directly proportional to the external ambient air temperature. Once again we are faced with the old problem of predicting the weather!

Various methods are available which utilise 'historical' weather data to establish 'average' values. It is then necessary for the engineer to compare this data against a formula fitting the relationship between the system's performance and the external conditions. Then an assessment may be made of the energy savings for a typical year. Two such methods are the 'BIN' method (ASHRAE)* – analysing weather data on a cumulative basis – and the use of 'banded weather data' (CIBSE).

Once this has been established all that remains is to address the effect of all the pennies that are going to be saved. This is where it may pay a lot of budding energy professionals to learn a few accounting methods. Common methods to use are 'simple payback' and 'net present value'.

Checklist

- Monitoring and targeting
- Remember the basic principles for measuring efficiency
- The concept 'degree days' will help to establish a basis for measurement by taking climatic variations into account
- Consider the difficulties of measuring the efficiency of your air conditioning systems
- Establishing a monitoring and targeting approach

- Source choice and tariffs

Consider the pros and cons of the various energy sources:
- Electricity
- Gas
- Oil
- Coal

*American Society of Heating, Refrigerating and Air Conditioning Engineers.

- Opportunities and vulnerabilities

  - Applications for combined heat and power systems
  - Prepared tariffs from interruptible fuel arrangements
  - You will probably gain most from ensuring that site personnel are fully trained and competent
  - Contract energy management can be a viable option

- Energy savings and initiatives

  - Building design: it is important to consider energy efficiency at the design stages
  - Cost savings are not always the same as energy savings
  - Take care when estimating payback periods in justifying modifications
  - Good housekeeping is probably the most important thing you can do
  - Review typical methods for achieving improvements
  - Use approved assessment methods for estimating payback

CHAPTER NINE

OFFICE SERVICES ————————

In an increasing number of organisations office services form part of the facilities management area of responsibility, either through direct management or via contracted out services.

In this Chapter we consider some of the common issues associated with office services functions and the topical contracting-out debate. Topics covered are:

- Raising the profile
- Strategic thinking for office services
- Sharing the vision
- Operational issues

Raising the Profile

All organisations rely on common core services in support of their principal business activities such as:

- post
- telephones
- records
- print
- fax/telex
- stationery
- courier services
- furniture

- storage and distribution   - travel arrangements
- reprographics

Office services can easily be neglected because of their low profile and, a bit like tap water, few people are concerned about how it gets there, only that it does. The effective management of these 'Cinderella' services is essential to the well being of the organisation. They are often the first point of contact that clients and potential customers have with the business.

Since there is never a second chance to make a first impression their performance can be critical. While the services are largely hidden, the results are not, and the effect of poor performance has an immediacy rarely felt in other business activity.

This is largely because many of the more traditional functions within office services are part of the organisation's communication structure, but they are rarely viewed in this way. For instance post, telephones, fax, telex, records, print, reprographics, courier services, distribution and so on are directly or indirectly supporting an organisation's ability to communicate with customers and staff. If they are badly organised the effects on business can be catastrophic.

Some organisations, especially in the finance sector, are renaming the office services manager as communications manager. This brings a new focus to the tasks and puts the management emphasis at a higher level. It also allows a broader view of the functions rather than a disjointed 'cherry picking' approach to office services.

Strategic thinking

Although many of the common core services operate to very short timescales, (daily, hourly or continuous services) they must be developed within the long-term strategic framework of the business. It is essential that managers responsible for these areas are well briefed on the company's primary objectives and how their functions fit into the strategy for achieving these goals.

For example, how often do you hear managers complain that their mailing systems, switchboards or warehousing are unable to cope with the substantial growth in their business? All too often, these situations are regarded as an unavoidable cost of success; 'growing pains'. The reality however, is that too often the growth is actually part of corporate goals and expectations but somewhere along the line, they have not been communicated effectively.

The office services functions are often forgotten in the overall scheme of things. The result is that managers of 'Cinderella' services are left working for today rather than planning for next month, next year, the year after. Is it any wonder that 'pain' seems inevitable?

Contingency Plans

Part of the process of strategic planning includes considering what contingency plans are necessary and how quickly they can be mobilised. The advantage of contingency plans is that the necessary thinking, research and decision making has taken place, all that is required is the decision to act.

A large in-house mailing unit found that volumes of work for a particular machine were far higher than anticipated. The machine was overloaded, backlogs and service failures were growing. Worse, the lead time for a new machine was 10 months, so potentially, the problem would exist for some time. Fortunately the company's contingency plans included a 'shell' contract with a third party mailing house. This enabled over capacity work to be shipped out immediately at a pre-agreed price and service level. *That* is the advantage of sound contingency plans.

Sharing the vision

With office services there can be a number of fairly mundane tasks so raising peoples willingness to achieve is of prime importance as a motivation factor. Sharing goals and objectives and your vision of the future will enhance your ability to achieve them. Consider:

Your staff. Help your staff to raise their sights above their day to day activity. Using the analogy of a bricklayer; if you can persuade your staff that they are building cathedrals rather then laying bricks you are far more likely to secure their commitment, loyalty and enthusiasm. Give them the information that allows them to understand where they fit in the grand scheme of things.

Your suppliers. Bring them into your organisation and show them how their equipment/services effect your performance. Make them feel part of your team. Tell them where you are going and ask them where you can help them, to help you to get there.

Your internal and external customers. Develop your aims and objectives with them in mind. Check continuously that where you aim to be is where they want you to be. Let them know how you are doing and where they can help you to achieve your objectives in line with their requirements more efficiently and effectively. Encourage them to visit your unseen 'Cinderella' functions and experience what you do. Increasing their understanding of what you do, how you do it and where you are going can only enhance and cement the relationship.

Operational issues

Office services encompass areas which are traditionally labour intensive – mailroom attendants, switchboard operators, central records or document retrieval staff and so on. The challenge for facilities managers running these areas is to ensure their clients receive an appropriate level of service whilst using the most efficient method of delivery. Today there are numerous options, whereas a short time ago direct employment of internal labour was the only solution. Advances in technology and the outsourcing fields in particular open up operational alternatives for office services.

Each service needs to be reviewed on a fairly regular basis against three basic criteria:

- Is the service level provided in line with user requirements?
- Can technology be used to increase service levels or reduce costs?
- Which employment method is most appropriate?

Service levels

Too often the service levels of today are relevant to the needs of yesterday. We've all seen computer reports that are produced every month and promptly filed never to see the light of day again. A manager once asked for the report, probably on an ad hoc basis, and it has been produced and never questioned for ever more. In much the same way, service levels can be hopelessly out of date.

A large electronics company employed over 20 internal postroom staff to receive, sort and distribute incoming mail. The office services manager conducted a survey amongst user departments and found that all received the same number of pick ups and drop offs every day. On further questioning it was found that different departments had different mail delivery requirements and instead of a uniform six drops per day some areas were content with one or two.

However, some who were directly driven by incoming mail did indeed require the six-a-day service. The changes, based on each departments actual requirements, resulted in a service level to each area commensurate with its needs and a significant saving in staff costs.

Use of technology

Virtually all the traditional Office Services areas have been exposed to technology development over the past few years. For instance:

Switchboard/telecommunications.

The advent of direct dialling facilities to internal extensions and the development of on-line directory systems have revolutionised traditional switchboard operations. Other features such as tele-conferencing, user directory on-line amendments, tie-line facilities and so on have all made an impact in this area.

Mailroom function

The biggest impact here is the advent of internal electronic mail systems allowing staff to correspond instantly via on-line terminals. This can drastically reduce the amount of internal paperwork and resultant physical distribution requirements. Other developments include – optical character reading equipment, intelligent mailroom equipment (envelope stuffers, franking machines etc).

Records management

A gradual movement towards computer storage of records via micro systems, optical character readers and so on has made enormous inroads to records storage and management. Even simple systems such as mobile racking and traditional microfiche are worth considering for certain situations.

Print and reprographics

This is an area where technology has revolutionised the industry and any facilities manager responsible for all or part of these disciplines should take trouble to familiarise themselves with the constantly ongoing developments. The main areas are – desk top publishing systems and intelligent photocopiers.

One blue chip organisation embraced a desk top publishing graphics system and reduced its studio complement from 15 staff to six whilst increasing output.

Employment methods

This area needs to be kept under constant review. Too often companies become locked into a particular employment channel especially in areas such as Office Services work where traditionally full-time in-house staff were the norm. Sound staff policies and labour flexibility are not mutually exclusive. Flexibility can fit particularly well into areas where workload fluctuations are experienced. For instance, consider:

- full-time staff
- part-time staff
- job sharing
- temporary staff
- short-term seasonal contracts
- flexible working hours
- shift working
- a mix

Achieving the correct balance will give the optimum service at minimum cost and enable you to react to changing demands.

Checklist

- Raise office service functions out of the Cinderella syndrome.
- Think strategically and tie in office services objectives to the organisation's corporate objectives.
- Develop operational contingency plans for each area.
- Share the vision with staff, suppliers and customers.
- Regularly review each service against three criteria:
  - Service levels
  - Use of technology
  - Employment methods

CHAPTER TEN

HEALTH AND SAFETY ────────

This Chapter is not intended as a detailed guide to health and safety. There are many excellent reference books on the subject which are commonly available from HMSO, the Health and Safety Executive and commercially available publications.

In this Chapter we look at the main issues of which to be aware and how facilities departments are gradually assuming more responsibility for health and safety in their organisations as their general scope increases.

We cover:

- The facilities manager's role within health and safety
- Main legislative framework
- Specific areas of interest
- Health and safety procedures for contractors
- Outline explanatory notes on relevant legislation
- The office environment
- Good practices checklist

Facilities manager's role within health and safety

In many large organisations health & safety is the responsibility of a specific department with wide ranging duties and management reporting lines within its own function. Board level representation is not uncommon, especially in safety critical industries such as construction, power generation, oil and mining. However, in some organisations health and safety is seen as a reluctant tag-on to existing duties and dealt with on a purely reactionary basis.

However, there is a trend which is bringing the management of health and safety issues into the facilities management arena. In recent years this trend has increased, and will no doubt continue, due to three main reasons.

Firstly, FM has been established as a recognised discipline where many health and safety responsibilities can be focused. Secondly, in response to the topical sick building syndrome debate, because of the source of potential problems – again mostly managed within the emerging FM areas – facilities managers have become heavily involved with analysing the problems and providing solutions. And thirdly, the European Commission Directives aimed at the working environment largely reflect FMs area of influence such as workstation design, office furniture selection, environmental comfort and so on.

The trend in legislation, both UK and European driven, is to concentrate on the specific rather than the general, eg detailed risk assessments and hazard identification. This is tending to shift responsibility to the 'specialist'. As facilities management develops into a recognised specialist role, so it will automatically attract extra responsibility for health and safety issues where these are not previously allocated. It is therefore important that facilities managers have a thorough understanding of the subject and know where to turn for further specialist assistance.

Within the diverse range of duties covered by facilities management, there is a need to define the relevant legislation having an impact on the areas of responsibility covered and identify the approach to managing health and safety effectively.

Specific areas of interest

Most facilities managers with health and safety responsibilities will need to be familiar with the following general categories of concern:

- A thorough understanding of the Health and Safety at Work Act 1974
- Building regulations
- Fire regulations
- Emergency evacuation procedures
- First aid training and equipment
- Legislation and guidelines specific to the particular industry
- Current and forthcoming European Directives on health & safety
- Principles of occupational health
- The organisation's health and safety policy document
- Health and safety procedures for contractors

The everyday responsibilities for areas such as office space planning, on-site contractors, provision of catering, window cleaning, lift maintenance, maintenance of air-conditioning systems, visual display unit operation, electrical appliance testing and so on, require a knowledge of health and safety regardless of who in the organisation holds the functional responsibility for health and safety. Of course everyone under the 1974 Act has responsibility to some degree, for ensuring work is carried out in a safe manner.

Knowing where to turn for assistance and guidance is important, especially for the smaller organisation where full-time health and safety officers are a rarity. Useful sources of information include:

- British Standards Institute
- Trade union health & safety departments
- Universities
- Commercial safety consultants
- Specialist commercial information providers (eg Barbour Microfile Index)
- Health and Safety Executive – Inspectorate, Guidance Notes, Codes of Practice
- Journals
- Text books
- Actual legislative documents

Main legislative framework

The primary legislation is the Health and Safety at Work Act 1974 and the two earlier statutes which are still in force – the Factories Act 1961 and the Offices, Shops and Railway Premises Act 1963. Some of the other major statutes in force are:

Fire Precautions Act 1971
Employment Medical Advisory Service Act 1972
Industrial Diseases (Notification) Act 1981
Food Act 1984
Occupiers Liability Act 1984
Public Health (Control of Disease) Act 1984
Food and Environment Protection Act 1985

Fire Safety and Safety of Place of Sport Act 1987
Petroleum Act 1987
Environment and Safety Information Act 1988
Water Act 1989
Control of Pollution (Amendment) Act 1989
Control of Smoke Pollution Act 1989
Employment Act 1989
Food Safety Act 1990
Environmental Protection Act 1990

Important Regulations include:

Protection of Eyes Regulations 1974
Health and Safety (First Aid) Regulations 1981
Reporting of Injuries, Diseases and Dangerous Occurrences Regulations 1985
Control of Substances Hazardous to Health Regulations 1988
Electricity Supply Regulations 1988
Electricity At Work Regulations 1989
Health & Safety Executive Construction (Head Protection) Regulations 1989
Noise At Work Regulations 1989
Pressure Systems and Transportable Gas Containers Regulations 1989
Health and Safety Information for Employees Regulations

European Commission health and safety Directives are having a big impact on certain areas relating to facilities management. For example – furniture, workplace layout and visual display units. The Framework Directive (89/391/EEC) concerns itself with the introduction of measures to control and improve health and safety of employees at work. The 'daughter Directives' include:

- Workplace Directive
- Use of Work Equipment Directive
- Use of Personal Protective Equipment Directive
- Manual Handling of Loads Directive
- Display Screen Equipment (VDU) Directive
- Carcinogens Directive

Health and safety procedures for contractors

Often, a large part of a facilities manager's responsibility is to employ and control contractors to work on site, either in a temporary capacity such as maintenance or refurbishment staff or permanently as in the case of security and catering staff.

In addition to statutory obligations it is useful for an organisation to devise common sense rules of its own to establish and maintain a high standard of safety for contractors whilst on its premises. These can be incorporated in the standard terms and conditions of trading or in model contracts.

The objective should be to ensure that contractors adopt safe systems of work which will not endanger the organisation's employees, members of the public, their own staff, or any other contractors' employees. Any additional document, such as a commercial contract, should not be regarded as reducing in any way the contractors own statutory obligations and common law duties.

A useful five point guide is:

- Build health and safety procedures/responsibilities into the contract
- Supply contractors with your own Health and Safety requirements in writing and check their understanding. A copy of your organisation's policy document will help.
- Ask for contractors' own on-site procedures and guidelines.
- Build in the right to inspect and monitor contractors' safe working practices
- Make sure appropriate training is available on both sides.

Outline explanatory notes on relevant legislation

The following notes are included as general comment only on the relevant legislation in order to give a 'flavour' of the subject matter within each area of concern. You are strongly advised to obtain full copies of the legislation documents via HMSO/HSE if you require further information.

Principal legislation

Health and Safety at Work Act 1974

The Heath and Safety at Work Act is the primary piece of health, safety and welfare legislation, and enables the responsible Minister to make Regulations to improve occupational health and safety.

The Health and Safety at Work Act requires that employers ensure, so far as is reasonably practicable, the health and safety of employees and others who may be affected by what they do, or fail to do. Employers have duties towards people who:

- Work for them, including casual workers, part-timers, trainees and sub contractors.
- Use workplaces provided by them.
- Are allowed to use equipment provided by them.
- Visit their premises.
- May be affected by their work.
- Use their services.

The Health and Safety at Work Act applies to all of the work premises and activities and everyone at work has responsibilities under the Act – employee, supervisor, manager, director or self employed.

The general duties of the Act are set out under section 2 and are as follows:

- to provide and maintain safe plant and systems of working
- arrangements for the use, handling, storage and transportation of articles and substances
- provision of information, instructions, training and supervision
- maintenance of a safe place of work and means of access to and regress from it
- provision and maintenance of a safe working environment

This Act is supplemented by earlier statutes which are still in force, notably the Factories Act 1961 and the Offices, Shops and Railway Premises Act 1963.

The Factories Act 1961

Under this Act Parliament identified the potential workplace hazards and stipulated the minimum standards of equipment and operations necessary to control them. In general the Act imposes on the employer the responsibility to secure the health, safety and welfare of their employees.

The Offices, Shops and Railway Premises Act 1963

The general requirements of the Act puts an obligation on the employer to provide a satisfactory working environment in respect of such matters as:

- cleanliness
- overcrowding
- temperature
- ventilation
- lighting

- sanitary conveniences
- washing facilities
- drinking water

The Protection of Eyes Regulations 1974

These regulations detail the responsibilities of employers and employees, to provide and wear suitable eye protection. Eye protectors can mean goggles, visors, safety spectacles and face screens, whichever one of these is considered appropriate for the specific task.

The Electricity Supply Regulations 1988

The Electricity Supply Regulations 1988 impose requirements regarding the installation and use of electric lines and any apparatus associated with the supply of electricity including provisions for connections with earth. These Regulations are administered by the Engineering Inspectorate of the Electricity Division of the Department of Energy.

The Control of Substances Hazardous to Health Regulations 1988

The Control of Substances Hazardous to Health Regulations 1988 became law as from 1 October 1989, in respect of all new work activities, and on 1 January 1990 in respect of all existing work activities.

The COSHH Regulations require an employer to:

- Conduct an assessment of substances used or generated in the workplace by relating to all situations in which they are used and the employees who use them.
- Control the exposure of employees to those substances by means ranging from elimination of their usage to satisfactory ventilation and personal protection.

- Ensure the use and maintenance of the control measures and adequate testing and examination is performed.
- Monitor the workplace atmosphere and conduct health surveillance on employees where appropriate.
- Inform, instruct and train employees on the risk created by exposure and precautions to be taken when using hazardous substances.

The Electricity at Work Regulations 1989

The Electricity at Work Regulations came into force on 1 April 1990. The purpose is to require precautions to be taken against the risk of death or personal injury from electricity in work activities. The Regulations are made under the Health and Safety at Work Act 1974, and impose duties on persons (referred to as duty holders) in respect of systems, electrical equipment and conductors and in respect of work activities on or near electrical equipment.

The Noise at Work Regulations 1989

The Regulations detail the responsibilities of employees and employers, to provide and wear suitable ear protection. Ear protection can mean ear muffs or ear plugs, whichever is considered appropriate for the specific task.

The Health and Safety Executive Construction (Head Protection) Regulations 1989

The Regulations detail the responsibilities of employees, and employers, to provide and wear suitable head protection. Head protection can mean industrial safety helmets or bump caps, whichever one of these is considered appropriate for the specific task.

The Pressure Systems and Transportable Gas Containers Regulations 1989

The Regulations place specific duties on users of pressure systems, who to comply with them will have to:

- Establish the safe operating parameters of their pressure systems.
- Provide a suitable written scheme for its examination.
- Have both these endorsed as satisfactory by a competent person.
- Arrange for examinations to be carried out by a competent person in accordance with the written scheme.
- Provide adequate operating instructions.
- Have a suitable written scheme of maintenance.
- Keep adequate records.

The Reporting of Injuries, Diseases and Dangerous Occurrences Regulations 1985

The Regulations impose a duty on the employer to report specified injuries, diseases and dangerous occurrences. The report should be sent to the authority responsible for enforcing the Health and Safety at Work Act at the premises where the case occurred. This will be either:

- the Health and Safety Executive for workplaces such as factories, building sites and farms
- the local authority Environmental Health Department for the area for workplaces such as offices, shops and restaurants.

Failure to comply with the reporting duty is an offence and is punishable under the Health and Safety at Work Act.

Health and safety information for employees' Regulations

The Regulations impose a requirement on the employer to advise employees about the statutory responsibilities under the Health and Safety at Work Act and other subordinate legislation.

This requirement can be achieved by:

— displaying prominently a notice in every workplace
— using a digest of the same information in pamphlet form to each individual employee.

The object of the Regulations is to make all employees aware of their rights and responsibilities. The notice/-pamphlet must provide the names and addresses of the local Environmental Health Department and the Employment Medical Advisory Service. Failure to insert the names and addresses is a breach of law.

The Health and Safety (First Aid) Regulations 1981

The Regulations require an employer to decide what provision is necessary for their business, taking into account the size of the workforce, siting of the premises and nature of the business carried out.

Having decided what is appropriate the arrangement must then be communicated to all employees. This can be achieved in a number of ways:
information can be displayed on company notice-boards; as part of the new starter induction programme; through the company health and safety policy document.

All first aid facilities should be clearly marked, and all named first aiders must have passed an approved course. Where staff numbers do not warrant the appointment and training of a first aider, an appointed person should be assigned, whose duties will include:

— taking charge in the event of an accident
— calling the doctor or ambulance service
— responsibility for the first aid boxes

The Environmental Protection Act 1990

The Act is extremely wide in its scope, as the statute defines 'environment' as including the air within buildings.

The aim of Part 1 of the Act is to bring in a regime of pollution control. Pollution is defined in the Act as the release into any medium of any substance which are capable of causing harm to humans or any other living organism supported by the environment. Harm can be defined as where offence is caused to any of the senses, for example dust can harm the respiratory system or excessive noise the faculty of hearing.

EC Health and Safety Directives

The introduction of the Single European Act enables the European Community to discuss measures and adopt Directives setting down minimum requirements for health and safety at work.

The Directives may have significant implications for all facilities managers in terms of potential increased responsibility and the need to manage health and safety in order to minimise work hazards.

Framework Directive (89/391/EEC)

The Council of Ministers adopted the Framework Directive on 12 June 1989, which is concerned with the introduction of measures to control and improve the Health and Safety of employees at work.

The Framework Directive is presented in two main sections, which cover employers' and workers' obligations. In addition the Directive already has a number of associated EC Directives and additional Directives have been drafted as well as proposals for future ones. These associated EC Directives are generally referred to as 'daughter Directives'.

Daughter Directives

A number of daughter Directives have been adopted and these are as follows:

Workplace Directive (89/654/EEC)

The Directive places the following responsibilities on employers:

- exits and corridors must be kept clear
- a clean workplace must be provided
- regular maintenance checks must be carried out on the building structure and M & E plant
- to provide a good working environment ie ventilation, temperature, lighting, washroom and toilet facilities
- fire safety/evacuation procedures

Use of Work Equipment Directive (89/655/EEC)

The Directive places the following responsibilities on employers:

- any tools used must be of good quality and suitable for the use intended
- all machinery must be suitably guarded and regularly maintained
- procedures must be in place to ensure that safe working practices are adhered to
- hazards such as fire, discharges of gases or dust, contact with live electrical equipment, exposure to legionella etc, must be prevented

Use of Personal Protective Equipment (89/656/EEC)

This Directive relates to the issue and use of personal protective equipment in situations where risks cannot be eliminated or reduced to an acceptable level.

The Directive places the following responsibilities on employers:

- to carry out risk assessments in order to identify requirements

- to select appropriate personal protective equipment and to supply it free of charge
- to ensure that staff wear the protective equipment when and where specified and to ensure that it is in good working order
- to provide information instruction training and demonstrations in the use of the personal protective equipment supplied
- to carry out regular auditing of noise levels

Manual Handling of Loads Directive (89/269/EEC)

This Directive relates to the issue and use of personal protective equipment in situations where risks cannot be eliminated or reduced to an acceptable level.

The Directive places the following responsibilities on employers:

- to carry out risk assessments in order to identify requirements
- to select and supply free of charge appropriate personal protective equipment
- to ensure that staff wear the protective equipment, when and where specified, and to ensure that it is in good working order
- to provide information, instruction, training and demonstrations in the use of the personal protective equipment supplied
- to carry out regular auditing of noise levels

Manual Handling of Loads Directive (90/269/EEC)

This Directive concerns itself with ensuring that risks of back injuries are minimised by careful consideration of all lifting tasks. There will be no 'benchmark' maxima for weights, either as to the weight, or by gender. This is because member states acknowledge that factors include the physique of employees of both sexes, and size and shape (as well as weight) of a load, the position from which lifting – and where the load is to be placed.

The Directive places the following responsibilities on the employer:

- to assess all manual handling operations taking into account factors including size of load, physical effort required, working environment and nature of the job
- to consider factors such as design of containers to ensure that handles allow a good grip
- to take into account the cumulative weight being lifted over long periods of time by each individual worker
- the results of fatigue, resulting in the loss of reaction speed in muscles
- the positioning of apparatus and equipment to overcome posture problems
- to train staff in correct lifting techniques

Display Screen Equipment (VDUs) Directive (90/270/EEC)

This Directive applies to all work stations with a display screen (visual display unit).

The significant requirements of the Directive are:

- all display screen workstations to be evaluated against certain health and safety criteria; appropriate remedial measures to be taken when criteria not met. Standards related to display screens, keyboards, furniture, lighting, working environment, task design and software
- workers to receive information and training and should be encouraged to take active participation in problem solving
- daily work on VDUs to be planned such that it is interrupted periodically by breaks or changes in activities
- workers are entitled to an eye and eyesight test before starting work with VDUs and at regular intervals thereafter, and if they experience visual difficulties. Workers will be entitled to an ophthalmological examination if the eye tests show this to be necessary, and they must be provided with special spectacles if these are needed for their work and normal ones cannot be used. The 'reasonable' cost of the spectacles will be met by the employer.

Carcinogens Directive (90/394/EEC)

This Directive covers the protection of workers for the risks related to exposure to carcinogens at work.

The Directive places the following responsibilities on employers:

The need to carry out detailed assessments of health risks created by work involving substances hazardous to health. The results of each individual assessment should include details of

- the nature of the hazard and the nature and extent of exposure
- whether substitution by less hazardous substances is reasonably practicable
- the control measures to be applied to prevent or reduce exposure
- operating and maintenance instructions and procedures, where relevant to ensure that exposure is minimised
- precautions under non routine conditions, including emergencies
- use of personal protective equipment
- monitoring procedures
- health surveillance procedures
- the need to record assessment and the results of the assessment, where carcinogens are involved
- to provide the appropriate health surveillance, unless exposure is not significant

Temporary Workers Directive (91/385/EEC)

This Directive is applicable to all temporary workers, such as:

- employees with fixed term contracts
- employees working through agencies
- any other class of temporary employee

The following responsibilities are placed on the employer:

- to be responsible for their health and safety
- to provide any necessary information and training
- to provide detailed job descriptions

- to provide them with details of the terms and conditions under which they will be expected to work
- to provide medical surveillance, when deemed necessary.

Future Directives

These will cover the following areas: working hours; pregnant women and working hours; biological agents; asbestos worker protection; safety signs.

The working environment

The facilities manager plays a vital role in the provision of a safe working environment. To provide an environmentally friendly workplace consideration needs to be given to the following issues:

Working with the design or acquisition team

There is a need to join the building design or acquisition team at the planning stage. Important decisions have to be made relative to the siting of the building to ensure that the full benefits of the site, such as natural daylight are gained. In addition the building form needs to be assessed with regard to space planning and energy efficiency.

For example, a shallow building plan enables full use to be made of the natural daylight and ventilation, whereas a deep building plan may need artificial lighting and mechanical ventilation, both of which increases capital expenditure and running costs plus has an affect upon the work practices within the property.

Sick building syndrome

Concerns over the health of the office environment has grown significantly over the past decade due to the volatile organic compounds used in the structure of buildings and in the internal fittings, furnishings and equipment. For example, the pollutant effects of two chemicals – benzine and formaldihyde – which are given off by photocopiers and carpets have a detrimental affect on the air quality.

In the majority of cases, if specific attention is paid to the design, construction and maintenance of the air conditioning system and careful consideration is given to the selection of the internal fittings and furniture, the problems can be minimised. In addition regular monitoring of air quality needs to be carried out to verify that the oxygen content is correct and that surplus carbon dioxide is being removed.

Lighting

Providing the correct level of lighting for the work task is particularly important both for psychological reasons and the prevention of eyestrain and general fatigue. Regular maintenance checks need to be carried out on all types of lighting and special attention should be given to fluorescent lighting in order that flicker affects are minimised.

Consideration should be given to combating the effect of fading daylight by the use of an automated lighting control system.

Temperature and humidity

The aims should be to create a pleasant and comfortable environment in which staff can operate effectively at all times, too high a temperature can cause exhaustion and drowsiness and too little can affect concentration and cause stiffening of joints and muscles.

Excessive humidity prevents the evaporation of perspiration and if the humidity level is too low it can aggravate respiratory and sinus problems.

Housekeeping

Good housekeeping practices play a vital part in keeping the workplace safe. All thoroughfares need to be clear of obstructions and fire exit routes need to be clearly indicated. Regular inspections should be carried out to ensure that all furniture and fittings are in a good state of repair. Particular attention should be given to the cleaning regime and a regular programme for carpet shampooing and window cleaning should be adhered to.

Electrical equipment and static electricity

Many accidents at work can be prevented if attention is given to the placing of electrical equipment and regular maintenance and testing is carried out.

Particular attention should be given to the prevention of trailing cables, the positioning of floor boxes and wall sockets, the overloading of sockets and the regular testing and inspection of all portable electrical appliances. In particular applications, considerations should be given to the provision of residual current devices to provide localised protection.

The build up of static electricity in synthetic materials, metal furniture and electrostatic equipment etc, should be prevented. Various earthing systems are on the market and the most suitable for the specific application should be utilised.

Control of substances hazardous to health

Within the office a wide range of substances and solutions are regularly used, some of which can be toxic to skin, eyes and mucous membranes. All substances which are hazardous need to be identified and logged under the Control of Substances Hazardous to Health Regulations (COSHH).

Lifting and carrying

Consideration needs to be given to the placing of equipment, furniture and miscellaneous goods. If any of these are badly placed which involves staff in heavy or awkward lifting operations there are considerable risks to back injuries. A good practice guide should be produced and issued to all staff detailing lifting practices.

Seating and furniture

Seating and furniture plays a major part in the provision of a pleasant and healthy working environment. Both should be selected carefully taking into account the needs of the job requirements.

The use of a specialist in ergonomics can often pay dividends.

Emergencies and emergency procedures

All emergency procedures should be regularly reviewed and especially so if layouts have been altered in any way.

Staff should be made conversant with evacuation and first aid procedures. Disaster recovery plans should be produced. These should be seen to assist management in such a way that if disruption to normal work activities occur, there will be minimum disruption and rapid recovery.

Visual display units

Using a visual display unit and associated keyboard has become an integral part of many jobs. With careful planning of the workstation it should be possible to provide an ergonomically correct design, whatever the physical size of the operator.

Some useful pointers in arriving at a comfortable position are:

- Movement is desirable but repeated over-reaching or unreasonable stretching is not (eg documents too far away or to view).
- Wrists should not be bent up or sown at extreme angles when operating the keyboard. It is also important not to twist the wrist sideways to reach the outer keys – the wrist should be moved over.
- The eyes of the operator should be approximately at the top of the screen level. This ensures that the neck is not included too far up or down when viewing the screen.
- If the operator is below average height and the feet do not reach the floor when seated, a footrest should be provided.
- Work closely with the operator to make sure that a comfortable workstation is achieved.
- Provide the correct desking and seating
- If the operator keys regularly from a source document it may be useful to provide a document stand.

Training

To fulfil the requirement of section 2 of the Health and Safety at Work Act, employees at all levels need to be adequately trained to carry out their duties. It is particularly important that details of training given and received are documented, given that a legal duty is placed upon employers to provide suitable training.

There should also be an ongoing training programme to cover repeat training at regular intervals, training to keep abreast of changes in legislation and training for staff who are promoted or who are moving into new areas of responsibility.

In addition, specific training needs to cover:

- staff joining the organisation
- young people
- temporary staff
- contract staff.

Checklist

- Become familiar with the requirements of the respective mandatory health and safety legislation and ensure that it is complied with.
- Set up good lines of communication whatever the direction (downwards, upwards or laterally).
- Ensure that staff receive suitable training and that documented records of training given/received is recorded.
- Issue contractors with a booklet detailing the health and safety requirement with which they must conform and ensure that they provide a 'methods statement' prior to the commencement of any work.
- Become familiar with the requirements of the EC Directives both current and the future ones that are on the statute book. Implement the requirement of the Directives as appropriate.
- Work closely with the design or acquisitions teams at the planning stage and ensure that they are aware of facility requirements when new/ refurbished buildings are to be acquired.
- Prevent sick building syndrome by good work practices and the careful selection of furnishing and fittings. Regularly monitor the air quality to verify that the oxygen content is correct.
- Provide the correct level of lighting for the work task

and combat the effects of fading daylight, preferably by automatic means.

- Ensure that the temperature and humidity within the office is kept at the correct levels and regularly monitored.
- Keep all thoroughfares clear and pay particular attention to the cleaning regime and general housekeeping.
- Provide a safe and secure place of work, seek advice from the police or security specialist, when necessary.
- Ensure that the statutory tests are carried out on electrical circuits and portable electrical equipment. Prevent the build up of static electricity by careful selection of furniture, carpets etc and use earthing systems on electrostatic equipment.
- Carry out an assessment of all substances and solutions which are regularly used and ensure that they are logged and identified.
- Issue a good practise guide to staff relative to lifting and carrying duties.
- Provide good quality seating and furniture which has been selected to suit the specific job requirements.
- Introduce a smoking policy using a tactful management approach.
- Review emergency procedures on a regular basis and ensure that staff are conversant with both fire evacuations and first aid procedures.
- Produce a disaster recovery plan so that should a disaster occur, there will be minimum disruption and rapid recovery.

CHAPTER ELEVEN

BUSINESS RELOCATION ——

Because facilities managers are primarily concerned with buildings and services it is likely that responsibility for all or part of a relocation exercise will fall within the remit of the job. Recent surveys have revealed that at any one time around 8% of businesses are either moving or contemplating a move. Sometimes this is in the form of an on-site development or physical long distance relocation.

In this Chapter we consider:

- the reasons for business relocations
- project management of a move
- 'D-Day' – the actual move
- do's and don'ts
- an opportunity for change

Reasons for business relocations

Regardless of the economic climate organisations are always on the move. True, the rate may slow down during hard times and quicken during boom years,but there will always be a substantial base of movement in the commercial field. Even in times of economic downturn, organisations who are financially able will be looking for property 'bargains' and those under pressure or down sizing may be looking to acquire reduced space or move to cheaper rental areas.

It is not always the whole organisation that will be relocating eg, individual offices, branch locations, regional depots, or operating divisions. The biggest relocations over the past few years have been service companies and in particular banks, building societies, financial organisations and insurance companies. Recently these have been joined by. some areas of the public sector who have been mandated to work on a more commercially aware basis.

In recent years the main reasons for relocations have been:

- Financial
- Labour cost savings
- Consolidation
- Provision for expansion
- Locational efficiency
- Shortage of suitable office space
- Labour availability
- Labour welfare

In simple space terms it can cost £120 per year just to place a waste paper bin alongside a desk in prime office locations. Example costs such as this tend to concentrate an organisations mind.

Project management of a move

Most organisations are inexperienced when it comes to relocation exercises and lack staff with the relevant professional skills to successfully project manage a complex and important task of this nature.

Given that a major relocation exercise is a significant milestone in an organisation's life and the consequences of getting it wrong can be catastrophic, the appointment of a project manager with specific responsibilities should be considered as early as possible in the decision process - preferably at the feasibility stage.

The overall objective for the relocation manager should be to interpret the organisation's brief, effect the relocation within budget limitations and without disrupting core business activity.

Here we deal specifically with the commercial aspects of a move. Other issues, such as staff relocation is, or can be, a separate project utilising specialist skills. There are numerous staff relocation companies who deal with staff mortgages, house purchase, new area visits, family counselling and so on. It may help to consult such a company if your organisation is moving all or key staff, especially if it is a first time experience.

The project manager will need to consider all or most of the following issues in the early stages:

- *Location* is an important aspect which will probably be dictated by various business considerations and a directive from your Board or partners. However, it may be appropriate for you to introduce certain Property Management aspects to your senior management which may influence the location decision.

- *New building specification* may be determined by:
    - staff numbers – and hence space needs – relative to business projections
    - space guidelines
    - IT requirements
    - General facilities (restaurants, filing, storage)
    - Special environments (computer suites, training rooms).

- *New site survey.* This is a must as soon as the new site becomes known. In the case of taking existing space it is essential to confirm aspects such as – raised floor dimensions, the floor grid arrangements, cabling provisions, air conditioning (or alternatives), access points, fixed partitioning restrictions, common services siting, lift reliability and so on.

- *Detailed space planning* with regard to current requirements, future staff growth/retraction, function changes and so on. (Refer to Chapter 3).
- *Refurbishment*
- *Fit Out*
- *Lead times* for critical services such as telecomms procurement. A critical path analysis exercise is essential at the outset of a relocation project to identify activities and/or suppliers of essential services on the critical path.
- *Removal contractors* should be selected and taken on board as soon as possible. They are a fund of practical knowledge and getting to know your contractor early can pay dividends.
- *Furniture systems* need to be sourced as early as possible especially if new systems are to be used.
- *Relocation consultants*, preferably with a facilities management background, can be used to good advantage and certainly in the case of the first time mover. Again, having them on board as early as possible will pay dividends.
- *Computer installations* need careful planning and close liaison with the appropriate operators or data processing departments is required.
- *Security systems* often require long lead times, not just for installation, but more importantly for testing. Make sure you cover this issue early on if your organisation is using a sophisticated system.

There can be a whole host of activities which need to be anticipated early on in a relocation exercise. The secret is to have one person responsible for all commercial aspects of the move and for that person to appoint a team consisting of members from the relevant areas. A typical team would comprise of staff from the following areas:

Team leader (preferably an FM person)
Computer specialist

Telecomms/data specialist
Removals contractor
Representative from a 'user' area
Personnel
Premises (surveyor, building technician)

Anyone relevant to the business activity with a critical interest in the move being carried out effectively should be included, eg a representative from computer operations.

'D-Day' – the actual move

On the day of the move there is probably a great temptation to cross fingers and hope that everything goes according to plan – and, of course, the plan is the crux of the matter. Success on the day depends not on luck, but on the work put in beforehand. Relocating a commercial office, however large or small, should be a series of carefully structured events.

Selecting a move contractor

This is a critical decision. A commercial move contractor should be appointed as early as possible, and ideally be involved with you in the planning, especially on moves which involve specialist areas such as laboratories, large hard-copy filing systems or sensitive computer hardware. It is worthwhile emphasising the need to not necessarily go for the cheapest, but appoint the most competent contractor and the one you can best work with.

This last point is essential. You need to be thinking 'on the same wavelength' and working as a true team. There is nothing worse than find out you have made the wrong decision during a time-critical relocation exercise, especially when the inevitable hiccups arise in the heat of a move. Get potential contractors to talk you through the details of your move as they see it. Do not rely on a description of someone else's project or a text book move. Ask for details such as crate labelling systems, floor plan notations and the mechanical handling devices likely to be used.

Consider all alternatives

The move plan, especially the timing of the move, needs to reflect the organisation's business criteria. For instance, can the company cope with a 'one-hit' move, especially if this is likely to take many days? This can be the cleanest way of ensuring a successful move, but some organisations may not be able to cope with the down-time it involves.

Consider a rolling move of different buildings or departments over an agreed timescale, where each move can be compartmentalised and treated as a separate project. Another alternative could be a weekends-only move where normal Monday to Friday operating hours are left untouched. There are other alternatives such as night moves.

Whichever system is selected, it needs to reflect the business criteria of the organisation – and always build in a contingency to take account of the unforeseen. This should be published as part of the move plan.

'D-Day' arrives

Here are just some of the pitfalls you can encounter on the day itself - if you have failed to plan the project well.

Police and local authority permissions

Make sure you have been in contact with the appropriate authorities well in advance for issues such as permission for removal lorries and staff vehicles to park on double yellow lines, or to cone off certain areas for loading and unloading purposes. There may even be a need to block off a whole street depending on the transport and access arrangements you require.

Lift maintenance

If you are using lifts in the old or new premises make sure there are standby arrangements for engineers to be on site or on a guaranteed minimum call-out time basis. Always ensure that lifts are well protected by temporary cladding, this also applies to heavily used walkways. Always comply with lift weight restrictions as there can be a temptation by over zealous contractors to squeeze one more item in. If you are relying on anything electrical or mechanical during your move ensure that you have alternatives readily available.

Access dimensions

It is vital that any limiting access points are measured prior to the move and checked against items having to pass through them. Critical areas are internal lift dimensions, main door heights and widths, canopy heights for vehicles and special arrangements for revolving doors.

Keys

Check well in advance that spare keys are available at both ends of the operation.

Legal possession

There cannot possibly be a problem here-or can there? If you are planning to arrive at eight in the morning it can be frustrating, if not disastrous, to learn on the doorstep that you do not have legal possession until midday. Check it out.

Site communications

If you are involved in a complex move with a number of key staff on different sites, they must be able to communicate. You will need to consider radio or portable telephone contact.

Waste clearance

Ensure there are adequate arrangements for the clearance of waste during the move. For instance, the unpacking of new equipment and protective materials around furniture can generate an enormous amount of waste which needs to be disposed of quickly and efficiently. It may be necessary to hire skips and therefore to get prior permission from the local authority to place these in temporary locations.

Health and safety

A major relocation exercise is a fertile ground for accidents. Make sure that someone away from the main stream of project planning is responsible for covering these aspects. For instance, fire extinguishers should not be used as door stops and hose systems should be turned on and tested before the occupation of a new building.

Additional insurance cover may be required over the specific move period if your main company insurance is not adequate. Always check.

Power

Ensure that all power and main services are on, especially in the new premises, and any handover arrangements or meter readings are completed before the building is vacated. You need to have a contingency plan for power failure during a relocation. If power loss is a critical factor consider hiring standby generators.

Catering

This is particularly relevant if you are engaged in round the clock shift working. Do you have any catering arrangements in place for both your own move staff and contractor's staff? This is a worthwhile investment; hungry people work slower and make more mistakes.

Wash room facilities

This is often overlooked especially in the new premises. Ensure that all toilets will be cleaned and supplied with all the necessary items during the period of the move.

Cleaning

Arrangements will have to be made for a 'deep clean' at the end of the removal exercise. Staff arriving at their new offices expecting a pristine location will be dispirited if they find heaps of rubbish.

Telephone system

All communication systems will need to have been planned well in advance. This includes general data cabling, fax machines, telexes and the telephone system itself. The worst time to be worrying about such systems is during the hyperactive period of the move.

Security

Make sure that you have made provision for adequate security arrangement for the premises you have just vacated. You will also need to make arrangements for security clearance of contractors and move staff at the new location to reduce delays on site. This is especially important if it is a multi-occupied building. You do not want to waste valuable time on the day in sorting out security badges for staff.

Vacated areas

There is a natural tendency to concentrate thoughts and planning effort into the new location. Do not forget that you may have obligations to fulfil in the old location, especially if you have a landlord/tenant agreement in place. Make provision for any dilapidations clause. Having these pointed out to you while you are leaving the building is not the ideal time.

Photocopiers

A facility which is often forgotten is the office photocopier. Many photocopier suppliers insist on their own engineers moving the equipment. Moving some of the larger machines yourself can be risky, potentially expensive, and in certain circumstances render maintenance contracts null and void.

Labelling system

Most commercial moves will make use of crated loads, often with may thousands of crates involved. It is essential that you agree a crate labelling system that accurately reflect the floor layout plans. Check that every plan is marked with location identifiers cross referenced to crate numbers.

Key staff

Always appoint deputies to key supervisory staff in case of sickness or accidents which may occur up to the last minute. Also insist on named deputies from contractors.

Do not move 'rubbish'

Your move will be longer and costlier if you do not get all staff who will be moving to sort their desks and filing systems to make sure that you are not moving unnecessary items. These should all be disposed of before 'D- Day'.

Stationery

It will not be a disaster on the day, but it will be soon after, if someone has not planned far enough in advance for new letterheads, business cards, sales literature, and so on.

Relocation do's and don'ts

DO

- Communicate the important points of the relocation to *all* staff.
- Involve as many people as possible at the planning stage.
- Appoint the major contractors as early as possible in the project and learn form their experiences.
- Draw up a CRITICAL project network and project check-list at the outset and keep it up-to-date.
- Hold regular progress meetings with minuted action points for all staff involved.

DON'T

- Underestimate the planning lead times involved.
- Lose sight of the business objectives in the heat of a move.
- Cover up any potential problems. Get them in the open and thrash them out quickly.
- Be blinkered by the 9-5 syndrome. You have 24 hours a day, 7 days a week at your disposal.

An opportunity for change

No well managed company will make large investments in major projects, of any type, unless a significant measurable benefit can be demonstrated. One major project which often falls short of this criteria is a company relocation which will often only realise 50% of the potential benefits of the time, money and resource invested.

The reason for this is that not enough attention is paid to the opportunities for change that a commercial relocation can offer. Lower rents or improved property investment strategy are often the only perceived benefits. Significant as these can be other benefits are too easily missed or ignored.

Catalysts for change

The mere suggestion of an office relocation can send the most hardened manager into trauma. There are not many executives of large or small companies who have regular responsibilities for relocation. Most people who have to manage a move are doing so for the first time and responsibility can often fall on anyone from the managing director to the personnel officer, or the chief accountant to the office manager. The only relocation experience for most people, to use as a benchmark, is their last house move – and we all know what that can be like! However, despite this initially pessimistic scenario, commercial relocations can be the catalyst not only for a cost effective premises strategy, but can help bring about positive improvements for many aspects of a business.

Relocation projects should result in a better working environment for the organisation even if this is a result of down-sizing. Unless the wider aspects of a relocation project are handled by a member of staff conversant with the management of change, and the ability to seek maximum opportunities from change, the organisation will not derive the pay back it should get from such a major project. In addition, using outside experts in relocation planning can only enhance the quality results achieved. Facilities management practitioners are ideally placed to ensure they have representation on an in-house relocation team.

Business, social, and cultural opportunities

Working with a dedicated project manager or specialist relocation organisation will allow the day to day mechanical issues of a relocation to be handled off the main business track, whilst enabling the company management (hopefully with facilities management representation) to consider the positive opportunities for change offered by such a project. For instance, here are just a few examples of the opportunities to be considered.

Open plan versus cellular office

The ideal time to consider the effective use of valuable office space is before a relocation. Is the older cellular individual office still appropriate for the business needs?

Moving to open plan can save space and costs and foster good team working. Conversely some staff who have been working in an open environment may benefit from the availability of temporary or permanent closed office space.

Shared space and shift working

More and more companies are looking at the cost of dedicated workstations for specific individuals, ie, is it a luxury or a necessity? Shared work stations for salesmen or office shift workers are becoming more commonplace.

Telecommuting

With reliable communication links becoming available, many organisations will need to consider the pros and cons of home based working. A major office relocation is an ideal time to consider such an opportunity.

Standard work station layouts

The cost of moving departments within buildings can be very high especially if the company is prone to organisational change. Adopting standard work stations and floor layouts can reduce staff reorganisations costs by moving just the people not the equipment and furniture. A review of space utilisation and typical workstation layouts can save a company significant costs from its premises budget.

For instance a leading financial organisation recently reduced its space cost by £7 million over five years as a result of reviewing its workstation layouts and space allocation for staff. In addition it is possible to reduce the costs of physically moving staff by 70% using standard layouts.

Centralised services

The debate on centralised or de-centralised office services rages, eg, typing, filing, photocopying. However a move to a new location is an ideal time to review your requirements in these areas.

Contracting out

Contracting out non core activities can make sense for many companies, there are many well documented methods for reviewing contracted services. Relocation is a good time to review needs and costs.

Single status catering

It may be an appropriate time to consider dropping the boardroom dining area in favour of an open plan single status catering facility, or simply a review of the beverage vending systems in use.

Smoking policy

It is often difficult to introduce a smoking policy that suits all staff. There is considerable social pressure building on this issue and many organisations have a declared smoking policy. A change of location can be an excellent time to develop a new approach.

Flexible working hours

A change of office location can mean different travel patterns for staff. This may be the ideal opportunity to consider a system of flexible working hours.

Part-time working

Related to flexible working hours, and if relocation means new staff, the opportunity for changing the pattern of the working day or introducing more flexible working rosters is a possibility. Many organisations, especially those in the retail industry, are having to look seriously at this type of issue in order to attract the right level and numbers of staff.

Creches

The old premises probably would not permit creche facilities. If appropriate to your company staffing requirements, a relocation is a good time to consider creche facilities.

Motivation

There are many ways that a company can use its buildings to promote general staff facilities and increase motivation for employees. For instance, consideration can be given to individual kiosk area, quiet areas, rest rooms if appropriate, centralised or dispersed restaurant facilities, and some companies may take the opportunity to introduce facilities such as a gymnasium. Where competition for quality staff is high these type of amenities can provide a recruitment edge.

And finally . . . communications

Communicate the move details to everyone well in advance – again and again. Use any means open to you – posters, bulletins, memorandums and special meetings. Do not forget your outside contacts such as suppliers, the Post Offices, customers, and contractors. Ensure that those who need to know the detail are given it. You cannot 'over communicate' on a subject as important as a major relocation. Depending on the reasons for a move it can also be turned into a PR exercise for external consumption – but that is only if you have total confidence in the planning. There should be no need to trust to luck.

Checklist

- Always appoint a project manager to coordinate the relocation.
- Consider the use of an outside relocation specialist, especially if it is the organisation's first move.
- Communicate the issues as widely as possible.
- Highlight business sensitive issues, such as computer installations, telecommunication criteria as early as possible and monitor closely.
- Do not waste the opportunity for change.
- You cannot over-plan a move.

CHAPTER TWELVE

GREEN ISSUES AND THE WORKING ENVIRONMENT ————————

Green issues or environmental management has moved from the sidelines to mainstream business life over the past few years. Some well known organisations are a success *because* they take the environment seriously while in others, customers are voting with their feet and taking their business elsewhere. In this Chapter we look at:

- Facilities and the environment
- Setting up good practices
- Building fabric and services
- Company transport
- Waste management and recycling
- Communication and involvement

Facilities and the environment

The way you manage your facilities will determine the impact you have on the local and global environment. The increase in research and attention given to environment issues over recent years has shown, beyond doubt, that many business practices and processes are damaging to the environment in which we live.

While manufacturing companies have the potential to inflict major damage and are more likely to experience environmental disasters, large office-based companies can still contribute significantly to the world's environmental problems. Also, the size of an organisation is not an issue when considering environmental concerns. The principles apply to large and small organisations alike.

Running the business in an environmentally responsible way should be integrated into the normal business process and simply be another aspect of good management practice. Your staff will also probably become increasingly aware of green issues in today's environment and will expect employers to respond accordingly.

Environmental issues are complex. It is important to understand them and how they relate to your business. So why not set yourself the objective of taking environmental issues more into account? Don't wait until you are forced to do so by legislative change. Nor until a good head of consumer pressure has built up (by which time your customers may well be going elsewhere) or until something goes wrong.

Aim to be proactive and start to manage your facilities in an environmentally responsible way to help retain your competitive advantage, to generate positive PR, to be socially responsible and to actively manage change in your organisation. So how do you meet the challenge of incorporating green practices, cost effectively, into the management of your facilities?

Setting up

Gaining commitment

Introducing environmentally responsible practices cannot be achieved without involving the appropriate people in your organisation. Firstly, like all successful business policies, the initiative needs not just the support of senior management but to be led by a member of the Board. With environmental issues making a fundamental contribution to the long term health of your business, it is vital that they are integrated into the normal business process.

Next, it is important to involve those senior managers from across the organisation who have responsibility for processes and practices which, directly or indirectly, have an environmental impact. The assembling of an environmental policy or practice group, meeting on a regular basis, allows commitment to be gained at the earliest stage and ensures the business can make environmental progress in a structured and co-ordinated way.

To establish a common commitment among the group and increase understanding of the issues and how your business has an impact, you should consider some form of initial training or workshop facilitated by an expert with environmental as well as business experience.

Draw up a statement of intent

Before you dive into tackling specific environmental issues, you will need to draw up an environmental policy, or mission statement, to guide you in your future action. It is important that the effort and resources you put into greening your facilities management are targeted to focus on the real opportunities and co-ordinated to ensure efficiency of action and effectiveness of solution.

Your policy statement will demonstrate your commitment to environmental excellence and should be drawn up in such a way as to produce a flexible living document which can be updated as new developments occur and be referred to, as a guide, to keep your efforts appropriately focused.

Your statement should:

- outline your environmental intentions
- define a strategy for implementation of your environmental actions
- identify appropriate measurements to check progress
- identify means of communication to inform and involve your employees and your external suppliers and customers
- commit to meeting or exceeding industry standards and setting standards where they don't already exist
- commit to ensuring awareness and understanding of, and meeting, all legislative requirements relating to your business

Reviewing your business practices

Now that you know where you are going, through your policy statement, you need to work out how to get there.

You will have found that there are many procedures and practices in your organisation which have an environmental impact. But which have the greatest impact? Which are the easiest to resolve? Where is the greatest opportunity to save costs? Where do you start? It is important that from here on in you proceed in a way which is structured and co-ordinated, meets the objectives set out in your statement of intent and where your actions are prioritised.

To achieve this, a review should be conducted of all those business areas which have an environmental impact. This review can be given to an external agency, who will also be able to help you prioritise actions and give examples of best practice and developments in other similar businesses, or you can conduct your own internal review.

If the latter, it is important that you are honest and objective in recording details of your findings. One way of achieving this is to involve your internal auditors in the process, or work in pairs or small groups to involve managers in reviewing each other's practices.

It is important at this stage that the review is comprehensive and looks at all aspects of every process. Remember that what happens within your organisation may well be only a part of the environmental chain and, if you are to consider the environmental impact from 'cradle to grave', you will need to talk to your suppliers or customers to assess the full impact.

Once all processes have been reviewed, your environmental group can now consider the various impacts of your operation and decide how and where to starting improving your environmental performance. This process will need to be considered carefully and, at this stage, you may find that you need further information or help in deciding exactly how to address the various opportunities.

Implementation

To put together your implementation strategy, you will be faced with a number of questions eg:

- what are the costs of changing your practices and, indeed, of not changing them?
- how do you decide whether one environmental impact is more important than another?
- how much, and when, should you work with your suppliers and customers to address 'cradle to grave' issues?

Once agreed, your implementation strategy will need to be produced as a prioritised timetable of action. This timetable should include designated responsibilities so that all those involved in turning the policy into practice are clear in purpose, direction, timescale and required result. As implementation proceeds, new legislation, developments and practices will occur which will need to be incorporated into your plans. Your plan will need to be flexible and reviewed from time to time to ensure it is still sensible, meeting your objectives and appropriately prioritised.

Lastly, implementation of your environmental aspirations needs to include your employees. The more they understand the business reasons behind your environmental plans and are given the opportunity to be involved and take part, formally or informally, in effecting change, the more committed your workforce will be in helping you achieve your environmental goals. Communication, therefore, is crucial in terms of raising awareness and commitment.

Building fabric and services

Good building and services design plays an important part in improving your environment and reducing pollution. Building operations are responsible for more external pollution than any other activity. Energy production for space and water heating, lighting and air conditioning account for about 50% of the annual production of so-called greenhouse gases in the UK. Large scale use of CFCs – for example in air conditioning systems – also contributes to the depletion of the ozone layer and to the greenhouse effect.

Thus, decisions at the design stage of building construction or major refurbishment can have long-term consequences and it is important to have a broad understanding of the key factors. The Building Research Establishment can provide information to help you.

Site factors and building form

The re-use of existing sites helps to slow down destruction of natural habitats. Try to find a site which has previously been built upon or reclaimed. A building on a noisy or dirty site is more likely to need air conditioning than a similar building in a clean and quiet location. Shelter from chilling winds can dramatically reduce energy consumption and trees or nearby buildings will form windbreaks.

Also consider the benefit of direct sunshine when selecting your site and building orientation. Passive solar gain can increase heat load in the summer but reduce the need for heating in winter. By getting your strategy right you can reduce operational costs at little or no additional cost.

Excessively deep buildings need expensive air conditioning and artificial lighting. Low rise shallow buildings with large surface areas will suffer from disproportionate heat loss. Ideally you need compact buildings which are naturally well lit to minimise energy consumption. Lastly, remember that very tall buildings can cause increased wind speeds at ground level around the building. It is important to consider this aspect when specifying your site and the building design.

Materials

The dangers of using asbestos have been well publicised. Blue and brown products are prohibited although white asbestos may still be used, mainly in cement and friction materials. However, suitable alternatives now exist. Similarly you should avoid using lead based paints internally and externally. CFCs and HCFCs are used as blowing agents in the production of some thermal insulation materials used in building fabric and services insulation, but alternative products include mineral fibre or bead polystyrene.

CFCs

Chlorofluorocarbons (CFCs) contribute to the depletion of the ozone layer and to the greenhouse warming of the earth. The full implications are unclear but we believe that a depleted ozone layer, for example, will increase quantities of ultra-violet light reaching us and lead to different kinds of environmental problems such as skin cancer and reduced crop yields. Some building insulation materials and air conditioning refrigerants use CFCs. They are also found in soft furnishings, some fire extinguishing systems, foam packaging and foam backed carpets.

Air conditioning systems should be designed for refrigerants that pose no threat or have a very low ozone depletion potential. Emissions should be minimised by good design and maintenance to prevent leakage of CFCs. Adequate access and pump-down containers should be incorporated and leak detection equipment should be installed.

You should monitor your consumption rate and question the need for excessive top ups to your system. Look for alternatives to halon in your fire extinguishers. Carbon dioxide, water spray, foam and powder are available. Also discourage halon emissions during training, for example the use of BCF hand held extinguishers.

Timber and timber products

We all know that the destruction of the tropical rain forests is a major cause of environmental concern. Much of the deforestation is to supply the western world with hardwoods and this large-scale destruction is reducing the earth's ability to convert CO_2 into oxygen as well as causing soil erosion and flooding. The UK is Europe's largest importer of sawn hardwoods including teak, mahogany and sapele. About 40% of our plywood comes from the tropics, and we import over 2 million hardwood doors from tropical countries every year.

Your architects, designers and contractors should specify and order timbers from sustainably managed

212

sources. If hardwoods must be used for doors, window frames, furniture, toilet seats, filing cabinets, etc, then indigenous materials such as oak, beech or elm are preferable. Locating importers who can supply timber from ecologically managed plantations takes a little time and effort, but it is well worth it.

Very often, fast growing softwoods like pine, larch and spruce can serve just as well as hardwoods but one side effect is that they may be impregnated with chemicals to improve durability. Watch out for potential health hazards this treatment may cause. You should also encourage the use of 'organic' paints which are less harmful than the cellulose solvents used in synthetic paints. The 'Good Wood Manual' and the 'Good Wood Guide' published by Friends of the Earth give information on some alternatives to tropical hardwoods and the names and addresses of companies claiming to provide timber from sustainable sources.

Company cars/transport

Few people will deny that while motor cars are one of the most significant inventions of the last 100 years, they are also the cause of some unfortunate environmental side effects.

First of all, accepting that the one-person per car scenario is the worst possible, you should consider offering alternatives to your company car drivers – much of this advice can also be directed to those of your employees who have their own cars. These alternatives could include bicycles (an increasing number of companies and local authorities are offering bicycles for short journeys) or mopeds, walking or using public transport. However, as the car is such a convenient and comfortable means of transport, it is likely that you will need to find creative ways of encouraging your staff to take up these alternatives.

Such incentives might include season ticket loans, a cash instead of car option, secure sheltered parking for bicycles or restricted parking spaces to discourage car use. The location of your offices will also have an impact on the means of transport used to reach them, whether located out of town or in the town centre and bussing from popular residential areas to your offices should also be considered.

It may also be fruitful to hold discussions with your local authority or public transport companies, especially if you employ a large number of staff, to see if local public transport can be made more convenient, more flexible or generally improved to encourage more take up by your, and other local companies', employees.

It is most important to ensure your company car policy doesn't inadvertently discriminate against non-car users, or encourage car driving in place of other forms of transport. Perhaps you could relate personal contributions to mileage rather than a flat monthly rate, to discourage high mileage driving.

Further, you can encourage your employees to car share and, for those employees who only need a car for occasional business travel, providing a car pool is preferable to each employee having their own car. Once you have thoroughly investigated all ways of reducing the need for travel by car, you then need to consider the environmental aspects of running a car fleet if despite your earlier investigations and implemented alternatives you have decided it is still necessary.

In formulating a company car policy, you need to lay down restrictions or, more positively, incentives which encourage drivers to select cars which meet as many as possible of the following criteria:

– capable of taking unleaded petrol
– fitted with three-way catalytic converters
– are highly fuel efficient
– incorporate recycled materials into the construction
– do not use tropical hardwoods
– are built to last.

Waste disposal is also an important issue and tyres, engine oil, car parts, batteries can all be disposed of in an environmentally approved way.

Lastly, both from a cost as well as environmental point of view, it is important that your cars are regularly serviced to run at optimum efficiency. It can also be very worthwhile to educate drivers, perhaps through your company car guidance notes or other means, in how to drive cars for maximum fuel efficiency and minimum wear and tear.

On a separate, but related, point, a similar review should be carried out on any delivery vehicles you use and here you can also look at the co- ordination of long distance deliveries to similar destinations, avoid empty vehicles and use vehicles of the appropriate size for the majority of your delivery needs, perhaps hiring vehicles for occasional special deliveries.

The whole area of cars and transport gives very significant opportunities for both improving your environmental performance and saving costs.

Waste management and recycling

You should also consider your consumption of office products and materials and their disposal.

All products have a finite life but, unfortunately, many products these days are designed for short term use and subsequent disposal – 'the throwaway society'. Many products are also disposed of well before they have reached the end of their useful life simply because a new 'improved' version has become available – the pace of product development and aggressive marketing fuels the 'throw it away, get a new one' attitude.

Again, for cost as well as environmental reasons, the maxim by which you work when dealing with product disposal should be:

- avoid its use at all (eg provide information on VDU screen rather than paper
- use less (eg every piece of paper has two sides!)
- reuse it (eg turn wasted computer paper into scrap pads)
- recycle it (separate at source and send to recycling company)

If it cannot be recycled, then you should consider finding an alternative product which can.

Waste minimisation and recycling is an excellent opportunity to involve your employees in helping you implement your environmental plans. Within your offices, you can set up recycling collection points for glass/bottles, paper/cardboard, can/metals, plastic (especially cups) and even waste food and organic material (compositing). Such recycling initiatives will also provide some additional income to the company which could be used to fund further environmental activity. There is also an opportunity here to work in partnership with your local authority, waste recycling companies and local charitable or voluntary groups.

Many items of office 'waste', eg boxes, poster tubes, tins, plain paper, etc can be used outside the company by local schools and playgroups. You will also find that there will be a demand locally for secondhand equipment, furniture, fittings, carpets, etc which you no longer need.

Another way of avoiding the production of polluting waste materials is to review your purchasing policy and, for example, buy cleaning products which are non-toxic and phosphate-free (but are effective cleaners), batteries which are mercury-free, solar-powered calculators, other products which do not contain petroleum-based solvents and avoid plastics which contain cadmium pigments (to help produce deep yellows and reds) and only use pesticides, preservatives and weedkillers in and around your premises which have been thoroughly tested and have minimal environmental impact.

Another area for review is the amount of packaging you use as a company or that your suppliers use - is it necessary? Could it be made of more environmentally-friendly materials?

Lastly, as well as introducing waste material into the recycling chain, it is also important that you help to expand the market for recycled goods by using them yourself. Recycled paper, for instance, uses less energy, less water and chemicals and reduces pollution. The more recycled paper used, especially outside the company to your customers, shareholders and suppliers, the more it will come to be accepted that 'quality' paper doesn't need to be ultra-white virgin pulp. Quality will take on a new meaning and as recycled paper is more environmentally responsible, it will become more impressive to use it than not to.

Communication and involvement

You also need to communicate your environmental plans and give the opportunity for involvement to your employees, customers and shareholders, the general public, your local community and your suppliers.

Employees

The implementation of your environmental policy needs to be understood and owned by your staff for it to be effective. Opportunity for involvement from the start is crucial in formulating policy and the implementation plan as well as the ongoing process of turning policy into practice.

It will also be important for you to consider the education and training of your people in basic environmental concepts and priorities; consider offering a suggestion scheme to harness their enthusiasm and creativity. For those employees who have some environmental responsibility, it is important to build environmental objectives into their job descriptions and appraise their performance against them.

Customers/shareholders

Not only are customers demanding non-damaging products, they are increasingly requiring any of their purchases or dealings to be with companies who can demonstrate good environmental practice. Shareholders will increasingly seek out companies demonstrating sound environmental records as it will be considered that companies who have not taken this area of business seriously will be increasingly exposed and under threat.

A useful and effective way of dealing with external enquiries is to prepare a concise, informative and honest PR statement, describing current initiatives and successes and intended future action, preferably giving target dates for implementation.

The public/local community

Companies have an important role to play in contributing to the wealth and quality of life of their local communities. Without due consideration for environmental factors, you can easily have a negative impact through unsightly buildings, contribution to traffic congestion, disposal of waste and pollution of the local environment.

The local community, in their turn, are important to companies in providing general support and approval as well as a source of labour. It will be important, therefore, that as a business you minimise your environmental impact on the local community and engage your local authority, voluntary groups and schools in partnership activities to increase environmental initiatives locally and, possibly, to share facilities.

Contractors and suppliers

Be sure to take account of the environmental performance of your suppliers of goods and services. Ask for details of the potential environmental impact of their operations and be prepared to work with them to improve performance where appropriate. Aim to raise the awareness of your suppliers, influence their environmental standards and communicate your own position. Ask for a statement of their environmental practices as part of the formal contract and review this annually. These steps will demonstrate to your contractors and suppliers that environmental issues are important in your company.

Checklist

- Gain commitment
- Draw up your statement of intent
- Review your business practices
- Implement your action plan
- Understand key factors for new buildings and projects:
  - consider site factors
  - material
  - CFCs
  - timber and products
- Reduce reliance on cars
- Reduce waste and increase recycling
- Communicate to all those involved in your business

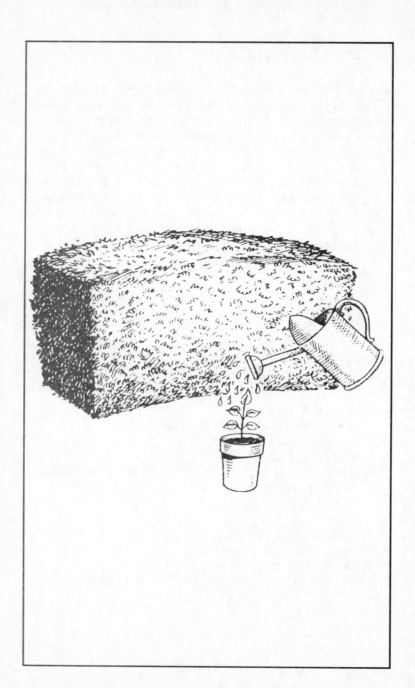

CHAPTER THIRTEEN

FACILITIES MANAGEMENT FOR SMALL BUSINESSES ————

The principles of professional facilities management hold good regardless of an organisation's size. Most of the material and ideas in this book will apply to small businesses even though they may not be set in the context of a large organisation. It is only the scale and apportioning of responsibility that changes.

We have included this Chapter on facilities management in small businesses to highlight the fact that FM costs are just as important, although relatively smaller, and that there are ways of addressing FM issues without diverting a disproportionate amount of time into the management of the costs.

In this Chapter we look at:

- The relevance of FM
- Cost grouping
- Apportioning responsibility
- A management approach
- Annual audits

The relevance of FM

There may be an instinctive reaction when discussing facilities management, to think the function applies only to large organisations. Specialist facilities staff, it is true, will not feature on a small organisation's payroll however, the constituent elements of property, equipment, power consumption, support services and so on certainly appear on the expenses of small businesses. These are common items to any business regardless of size.

If we take, as an example, a company occupying around 5,000 sq ft in a provincial location with average rent, business rates and service charges, the annual outgoings on these elements alone can amount to between £90,000 and £120,000 per annum. In London of course these costs would be significantly increased. Add to that the costs of power consumption (depending on business activity), extra service contracts, any catering arrangements, office equipment purchases, internal moves etc, and the facilities costs start to stack up as a routine yet significant element of running the business.

Cost grouping

The amount of time spent reviewing and controlling facilities costs will obviously depend on the size of expenditure and the sensitivity of the services to the main business activity. For instance, if water supply is critical to a production process the 'facility' will be monitored regardless of purchase cost. Likewise a company reliant on telesales activity will pay particular attention to its telecommunications facility.

Each service needs to be identified in an initial audit, sized and analysed. Individually, they may not be significant but grouped they could easily amount to a third of the organisation's outgoings. The likely range of items includes:

- rent
- business rates
- service charges
- electricity
- gas
- water
- cleaning

- security
- building maintenance
- plant or equipment maintenance
- landscape maintenance
- catering
- contract staff
- switchboard operations

Apportioning responsibility

It will be useful for one person in the organisation to be responsible for monitoring and managing the 'bundle' of facilities alongside the main role responsibilities. This need only take a small proportion of time available throughout the year. By 'bundling', the individual costs will not slip through the net, and the total creates an opportunity for tight control, management focus and savings.

A management approach

The basic option is to handle in-house or outsource to a specialist facilities management company. Handling the cost issues in-house will depend on the manager's time available, knowledge of the subject, enthusiasm for the task and issues of business security.

The alternative, contracting out facilities, need not be cost prohibitive. The options here are to pay:

- on a straight hourly rate basis
- an annual retainer or management fee
- a no fee shared savings basis

The latter can be very attractive to small businesses as it embodies the 'no benefits no payment approach' to consultancy. The only thing to watch here is the basis on which savings are calculated and the projected benefits period when a proportion of the savings are to be paid. Make sure you have a watertight agreement at the outset to avoid later misunderstandings.

Annual audits

After the initial project to identify costs, controls and savings, a cost effective way of managing facilities for the smaller business is to hold a diarised annual audit. This can be achieved in-house or via consultants depending on the management approach selected.

A small business often cannot afford a continuous monitoring or rolling audit approach, therefore the once-off annual audit is a disciplined way of reviewing the 'bundled' facilities. Each function will have a few key cost drivers to review. For example:

Power
- are the correct tariffs being applied?
- can certain processes be switched to off-peak periods (machines, laser printers, etc)?

Cleaning
- what are the local hourly rates?
- where is your contract relative to market rates?
- can you 'hitch' to a larger contract nearby?

Service charges
- is your landlord managing the services efficiently from *your* point of view?
- are there any services for which you are paying but gain no benefit?
- are there any services the landlord does not   provide, but in your opinion should?
- are you paying the correct proportion of the   building running costs?

Checklist

- Develop a structured approach to facilities costs
- Group all-FM related costs
- Make one person responsible
- Decide on approach – in-house or contract out
- Consider a shared savings contract
- Carry out an annual audit
- Review each cost driver for every service.

CHAPTER FOURTEEN

TQM FOR FACILITIES MANAGEMENT

Many organisations have now taken on board the concept of total quality management (TQM) in one way or another and it is known by different titles in various organisations – eg TQM, quality service, customer care, quality improvement programme, and so on. For this Chapter will we use the term TQM to embrace all quality led initiatives and methods of working.

The aim of this Chapter is to discuss the principle of TQM, then relate it to what has to be done within the facilities management field, how to do it and who should be involved.

This Chapter deals with:

- TQM history and definition
- How does TQM apply to facilities management?
- Implementing TQM
- Communications
- Supplier/contractor involvement

TQM history and definition

The power of a total commitment to TQM is easily demonstrated by the rise of Japanese industries in the major world markets since the early 1950's. To attribute all Japanese success to TQM is of course an over-simplification, however most management gurus and the Japanese themselves acknowledge that the cornerstone of their post war success has much to do with the adoption and total belief in TQM – the obsession with giving the customer what they want and continually striving to better current performance.

A good example of the power of TQM within a industry sector is the recent history of the worldwide semiconductor market. The Japanese were relatively late to adopt TQM in their semiconductor industries but when they did the results were impressive. In 1975 three of the top ten Semiconductor companies were Japanese and these were all in the bottom half. By 1986 this had increased to five with positions one, two and three all occupied by Japanese companies. In 1988 six Japanese companies featured in the top ten and they continued to dominate the top three places. All this was at the expense of America and European manufacturers.

Examples like this are often referred to as the 'Japanese Miracle'. Of course there is no miracle, just a commitment to hard work and an active desire to do better at *all* levels of the organisation.

Traditional management thinking has to change in order for TQM to be effective and to achieve sustainable benefits. First of all there has to be top level commitment to the concept, not just lip service to a new campaign. Secondly, management's role has to change from 'rule maker' to 'facilitator'. A useful phrase has recently been coined which illustrates the revised role – that is 'removing the boulders from the runway'.

It is essentially an enabling process. This means that the usual reporting pyramid showing board members and senior executives at the top with supervisors and workers at the broader bottom is inverted. We then get a truer picture of the senior managers within an organisation supporting the operatives – enabling them to carry out their work, with the customers at the top.

So *what* is TQM? Dr W Edwards Deming has contributed more than anyone to developing the modern approach to TQM and has helped shape this definition.

- QUALITY is continually satisfying customer requirements
- TOTAL QUALITY is continually satisfying customer requirements at least cost
- TOTAL QUALITY MANAGEMENT is meeting these requirements at least cost, through harnessing everyone's commitment.

So what is 'quality'? Deming states: 'Good quality does not necessarily mean *high* quality. It means a predictable degree of uniformity and dependability at low cost with a quality suited to the market'. For instance, the perceived quality of a Rolls Royce is obviously different to that of a VW Beetle, however both consistently suit their customers requirements and can therefore be said to be meeting a quality demand.

How does TQM apply to facilities management?

Facilities management is essentially a service to the core business of the organisation. You only have to think of the more usual functions under most FM departments responsibility such as cleaning, building maintenance, space planning, security, catering, engineering and so on, to understand that service to an internal or external customer is the raison d'etre. In this area relevant to the FM practitioner Deming raises and answers a common issue:

'In the service industry, most workers do not think they have a product. They think they just have a job. They do have a product . . . service'.

Satisfying customer requirements must be the main goal of every facilities manager. Customers expect quality because, they want a service that is reliable, they want it to meet their requirements and they want value for money. It is not a 'luxury', it is not meeting your own standards, it is agreeing what the standards are with customers and continually achieving them by encouraging everyone's commitment. Quality in facilities management means satisfying customer requirements, reducing costs by getting things right first time, and avoiding waste by eliminating errors. It does not mean doing things on the cheap.

Principles of TQM

The principles behind TQM which help achieve your customers' requirements are contained in six basic principles. They explain how TQM can be implemented and the 'rules' by which it is operated. The six principles are:

- The philosophy – prevention not detention
- The approach – management supported
- The scale – everyone responsible
- The measure – the cost of quality

- The standards – right first time
- The theme – continuous improvement

Using these six basic principles the facilities manager can ensure that the requirements of the customer are met at all times. Closer examination of each principle reveals how the facilities manager can apply them to help achieve a quality service.

The philosophy – prevention not detection

It sounds so simple, in fact everything to do with TQM is just that. However, there are many examples where detection has been the norm rather than preventing the error in the first place. Take the specification for a suspended ceiling calling for a fixed tile. If all the mechanical plant is installed above the suspended ceiling, it makes access for maintenance an extremely difficult and costly operation.

Another simple example is the siting of the waste bins in a kitchen area. If people have to carry used tea bags or throw them across the kitchen, the implications are obvious – stained floors and walls, disgruntled customers and shoddy work areas. No doubt you could think of more simple examples of actions that could have been operated more efficiently with some forethought.

The approach – management supported

The crucial word here is 'supported'. If the facilities team see TQM service as something they have to do rather than genuinely want to do, it will make the implementation much more difficult.

The facilities manager has to set the rest of his team an example on how to operate a TQM. The manager should be seen to support and motivate his teams by open communication and total commitment.

Quality service has to be seen as a way of life, *not a campaign*. The facilities manager needs to convince his people that it is the norm to question procedures, instigate change and talk to the customer. It needs high level management support so that the whole team can see TQM isn't just something imposed on them. They have to be convinced that the senior management have embraced and understood what TQM means.

The facilities manager should look to help, train and support his team to make their own decisions in their own areas. The team should be looked on as the front line in communication with the customer. It doesn't matter how good the facilities manager is, if the front line team are not communicating well with the customer, then a quality service cannot be offered. It is the process of 'removing the boulders from the runway'.

The scale – everyone is responsible

Everyone has to be responsible for delivering TQM. Even the people who may not have a direct contact with external customers should realise that their internal customers are just as important.

The facilities team need to look at the work they do and ask themselves the following questions:

- Is the job I am doing going to help my customer?
- Does the job achieve the standard I have agreed with my customer?
- Is the job necessary or am I doing it because it's always been done this way?
- Is there someone better able to tackle this task, giving them more responsibility and freeing up the facilities manager's time?
- How can I improve the job to increase the level of service I give to my customer without increasing the time taken or costs?

The recurring question should be: 'Am I taking responsibility for improving the quality of my work'?

The facilities team must look to continuous dialogue with their customers to ensure the standards they have agreed are being met first time. This is why it is so important that the front line staff have to take the responsibility to talk to their customers. An example of this could be:

- In a mail room area the standard agreed with the customer is that all incoming post is delivered by 09.00 hours each morning
- The customer is unhappy as the post seems to be delivered two hours late. The perception of the customer is that the service is bad due to poor delivery however, the front-line person, the postroom operative knows that the delay is in the customer's receiving area.
- If the postroom operative has the responsibility and takes it, he should start the process of communication with the customer and the facilities manager to redress the problem.

In this way the customer is made aware of a problem that cannot be resolved by the facilities team, but can see that the standard is actually being achieved. This example may sound almost too simple, but how many examples can you think of where someone hasn't taken responsibility at the outset and the service to the customer or the customer's perception of the facilities team has suffered? Of course it may be that the delay is in the facilities area of responsibility, in which case the service should be quickly reinstated to conform to customer requirements.

The measure – cost of quality

The cost of quality can be looked at in a number of ways. There is the short term view that cutting down on the external painting of say, softwood window frames is a saving but the long term loss is that the window frames need replacing earlier than if they had been maintained properly.

Other simple examples could include having to:

- Re-type a letter.

- Repeat any job not done properly in the first place.
- Deal with customer complaints about shoddy work-manship or poor service. Some organisations have large customer complaints departments. This is throwing money at the symptom not investment in eliminating the source of the problem.

All these examples cost money, which is money unnecessarily spent. If the job had been carried out correctly first time, there would not be any need for additional costs.

Looking at ways of improving a task can lead to enormous cost savings. Sometimes, it may be necessary to spend money up front with a view to recovering the investment later on through increased customer satisfaction.

Individuals should be given responsibility to look at their tasks and try to eliminate waste, therefore reducing costs even more. Given responsibility and delegated powers individuals will often respond by taking the initiative on costs.

The standard – right first time

'Do it right, do it right first time' is an old saying which facilities managers should still look to achieve.

The implications of not doing it right first time are:

- wastes time for everyone – customers and the facilities staff
- puts everyone under unnecessary pressure
- costs money
- makes customers dissatisfied with the service

No one likes doing a job badly. It demotivates them and customers when not performed right first time.

The theme – continuous improvement

It has been mentioned before that TQM is a way of life. It is not a campaign with an end result to be achieved before moving on. TQM never ends.

No matter how much we improve, our competitors will continue to improve and our customers will expect an even better service from us. Continuous improvement is about:

- reviewing all the services provided to customers on a continuous basis. Sometimes this can be daily such as the need to receive post at a specific time. Other times it can be done when a contract is ready for renewal.
- asking the question am I taking responsibility for the quality of my work and the work I receive?

Continuous improvement is perhaps the most fundamental and difficult part of TQM to grasp. After the initial stock of TQM ideas, we need to ensure that things do not fall back to old ways. This needs good management support. Continuous improvement emphasises the point TQM is a way of life not a campaign.

Implementing TQM

Management support

It has already been mentioned that the facilities manager has to be seen to set the example that the team can follow.

In many companies, TQM in one guise or another will already have started so the facilities manager should have help and support in implementing it. Sadly however, a lot of companies will not have started on the road to TQM, and it will be up to the facilities manager to start the process.

Almost all of the basic principles of TQM are just good management techniques. The problem is applying all of these techniques when you are inundated with work, when you have to work to extremely tight budgets and still keep your customers happy. It is precisely these reasons that make TQM an absolute necessity for today's facilities manager.

Quality circles

Quality circles are basically teams of people who work together and are empowered to improve the output of their team by identifying problems, investigating causes and providing solutions. The ultimate aim being to improve the service offered to customers.

These issues can cover diverse topics such as foot stools for switchboard operators, to identifying a way to get rid of a power generator by utilising other resources available.

It may seem that foot stools are not a quality issue, but look at it this way, if it helps the front line staff perform their job better at minimal expense, it will eventually see its way through as contributing to a better service for the customer.

The savings made by the removal of the generator are obvious. However, the not so obvious benefits are, it increases job satisfaction for the members of the quality circle, it shows they are thinking about ways of improving the service and helping to reduce costs.

The facilities manager should be seen to support the quality circles. They should be encouraged to implement their own ideas, particularly the ones that cost nothing and improve the service. The manager should also ensure that any of the points raised by the quality circle which they cannot answer themselves always receive an answer. It will be seen as one more example of the facilities manager supporting TQM.

Identify customers and clients

As facilities managers we may sometimes get involved with conflicts outside of our control. Where the client (the person who agrees the service and foots the bill) and the customer (the end user) seem to be at odds. An example of this could be:

236

- Air conditioning plant in a building. The plant is overdue for renewal. It is giving poor and faulty service. The customers are very unhappy but the client balks at the cost of replacing the equipment.
- Where does this leave the facilities manager? In a very difficult situation!

One solution is to make sure that the feedback to the client comes from the customers as well as the facilities team.

It is very important that the facilities team identify who is their client and who is their customer. Another example of the importance of this is where teams are taking instructions from customers who haven't agreed the service. This is an area where conflict can easily arise unless identification of who is the client and who is the customer has taken place.

Agree service levels and standards

This section outlines the service levels we agree with our clients and standards agreed with our customers.

- *Service levels.* This is the 'contract' between the facilities team and the client. It's the agreement to provide a certain service at a certain time in a certain way. The client is paying for this service (either directly through cost centre reporting or indirectly via overheads) therefore the agreement must be clear so that both parties know exactly where they stand.
- *Standards.* These are detailed working agreements between the front line facilities team and the customers (users). In many cases, service level agreements and standards are agreed together which helps understanding even further.

An example of service level and standards setting can be shown from this instance of a records management area in an insurance brokers. Records retrieval is part of the office services function which in turn reports to the facilities manager. The overall service agreement between the client and the facilities manager is that a records retrieval system will be provided between 8.30 am and 6.00 pm Monday to Friday.

The service standard agreed at customer level states that files will be provided within one hour of request and wrongly 'pulled' files will exceed no more than half of 1% of occasions during a month. The emergency service provides files within 15 minutes of request.

Improved service level agreements and standards are achieved by delegating these as much as possible to the front line team members. After all it is these individuals who are going to deliver the service and the more involvement they have the better the service to the client and customer.

Communication

Good communication is essential for quality improvement. Without appropriate communication, virtually all the other aspects of TQM will fail. Good communication is about:

- keeping the facilities team aware of what is going on
- keeping customers informed, especially if the agreed service levels are going to be difficult to meet
- ensuring understanding
- helping everyone work together

Supplier/contractor involvement

How do we get suppliers and contractors to participate TQM?

In most organisations the majority of the service tasks such as cleaning, security and maintenance will be carried out by contract labour. The question is, how do you get the contractors/suppliers to adopt a TQM approach which mirrors the in-house commitment.

A good start is to ensure contractors/suppliers have either achieved ISO or BS Standard 5750 or are in the process of gaining these recognised standards. These are fine as far as they go but cannot *guarantee* you will receive a quality service.

What needs to happen is an education programme similar to the one which was started with the in-house facilities team. Ensure the contractors/suppliers know what service levels have been agreed. The only way to ensure that suppliers/contractors deliver TQM in their work is to treat them as if they are part of the 'internal' organisation. Make them feel part of the facilities team (which they are).

The service levels and standards agreed between the contractor/supplier and the facilities team should always have a TQM basis. They should point out what is expected from the supplier/contractor and what is expected from the facilities team. This will go a long way to helping the suppliers/contractors buy into quality service.

Of course, at contract renewal stage when alternative contracts are being assessed, an integral part of the selection process should be to identify which companies already operate some form of TQM which aligns with your own approach.

Checklist

- TQM is a way of life, not another campaign.
- The principles of TQM will help outline the background to providing a quality service.
- Quality circles. The key to success. Get your team involved as quickly as possible.
- Service level agreements. These need to be in place to ensure everyone knows what is required of them.
- Communication. Another key to success. With good, positive communication everyone will have a greater understanding of how to deliver TQM.
- TQM is a way of life, not just another campaign.

CHAPTER FIFTEEN

PROPERTY AND LEGAL ISSUES

Some key legal property-related terms

In the introduction to this book and throughout the text there are many references to the fact that Facilities Managers come from a wide variety of general and professional backgrounds. This invariably means that most people are on a steep learning curve in at least a few areas under the diverse FM umbrella.

An area which often gives rise to confusion or the need for a basic understanding of terms and jargon is the property element of FM work. This of course is the province of the professional Chartered Surveyor, many of whom are also entering the Facilities Management discipline. However, for people entering from a different background, for instance Office Services or Engineering, a broad understanding of the terms usually encountered in property management will be useful. This short reference chapter has been included to cover high level explanations of the more common legal/property related issues.

This chapter deals with:

- Property ownership
- Leasing
- Statutory controls
- Uniform business rate
- Service charges
- VAT
- JCT contracts
- Building Regulations.

These are by necessity overviews and it is recommended that if further information is required professional reference should be used.

Property ownership

Most Facilities Managers would consider ownership to be when the organisation holds the freehold interest in its own property. On occasions the interpretation of ownership is extended to include where an organisation holds a long lease or ground lease of say 99 years or more on the property. In this situation a ground rent is paid to the freeholder, and because of the existence of a ground lease the organisation needs to be aware of its obligations to the freeholder.

Leasing

The UK has a well established property market which supplies organisations with space which they can occupy on a lease for any period from a couple of months to twenty five years. The lease is simply a contract between the landlord and tenant, and includes the amount of space to be taken, the rent to be paid, how the rent is reviewed and what are the obligations of each party.

The Facilities Manager needs to know the terms of the lease, in the same way as any other contract which the organisation holds. Much of the mystery of leases can be broken down by asking simple questions, such as how long does the contract run for, is there an opportunity for the tenant to break the lease, how can the company dispose of its lease and is there any restriction on the use of the premises?

In addition to what is stated in the lease, there is case law and legislation contained mainly in the Landlord and Tenancy Acts which also affects the basis upon which the property is held. A worthwhile investment is to instruct your solicitors to prepare a summary of all the leases held, and in a format that allows you to build up a property database.

Statutory controls

The Facilities Manager also has to be aware of the limitations which an organisation may have on its occupation of premises due to local or central Government legislation. The principal restrictions or guidelines are found within Planning Permissions, Building Regulations, Fire Certificates and of course the myriad of Health & Safety legislation.

Again it is worthwhile building up a database and understanding of how these controls effect your occupancy of a building.

The uniform business rate

History

The rating system in England and Wales underwent radical change in 1990, affecting both the basis upon which properties are assessed and the all important level of occupiers rate liabilities. To understand the effect of the changes, it is necessary to look at the system in place before 1990, when rating was subject to the provisions of the General Rate Act 1967.

Until 1 April 1990, properties were assessed on a rateable value derived indirectly from 1973 rents, to which a multiplier or rate in the pound, set by local authorities, was applied to produce an annual rate liability. The amount of rates payable in different parts of the country varied enormously depending on requirements and the policies of local authorities. As a generalisation, building for building in the late 1980's, rates tended to be high in the North relative to the South East as a proportion of rent.

The new system was introduced with the aim of redressing this situation and followed the local Government Finance Act 1988, replacing earlier legislation. Domestic property was removed from the picture, with general rates being substituted by the community charge.

For all commercial properties after 1 April 1990 the basic procedure for arriving at a rate-payable figure remains similar ie ratable value x multiplier, although these elements have altered fundamentally with the introduction of a new basis of assessment and the Uniform Business Rate (UBR).

Basis of Assessment

Rateable Value is now based on levels of rent as at 1 April 1988, dramatically increasing the assessments compared with the old system, particularly in the South East.

Multiplier

From 1990 the multiplier is set nationally and is known as the Uniform Business Rate. There may be slight variations in UBR between England and Wales and special provisions applying to the City of London although to date the UBR in the City has been set at the same level as the rest of the country. The UBR is increased annually in line with the Retail Price Index.

Vacated Premises

A saving on rates can be achieved if the whole of the accommodation within a single assessment is vacated and all furniture removed. Under the present system, rates will cease for a period of 3 months following vacation and then resume at 50% of the full liability for as long as the premises remain empty.

Transitional Provisions

Because of substantial increases, transitional arrangements were originally applied whereby the uplift was limited to 20% per annum plus inflation. Similar provisions were put in place to phase any decreases in liability, and these were limited to a 10% per annum reduction, but again with inflation added back.

The effect of this in the first year of the new system meant that large increases were phased at just over 29% whilst decreases were limited to slightly below 4%. Further changes have now been introduced to ease the burden of these transitional arrangements. In general, the effect will be to reduce the phased increases to an inflationary level, and accelerate the decreases for those where the revaluation brought about a reduced notional liability.

Phasing relief on increases will also now apply where there is a change of occupier, whereas under the original arrangements, a new occupier would have immediately assumed the full rates liability without the benefit of phasing.

Appeals

There are opportunities to appeal against a rateable value assessment. Such opportunities now only arise in limited circumstances and within strict timescales. Special advice should be sought having regard to specific circumstances.

Service charges

Traditionally, the type of lease favoured by the UK's institutional landlords passes a full repairing and insuring responsibility onto the tenant (the FRI lease). The effect is that the landlord receives rent exclusive of all other outgoings and passes on either a physical or financial burden for maintaining the building and the provision of its services. Tenants of self contained buildings in sole occupancy will therefore, in all likelihood, take on the responsibility for the building as a whole, maintaining the structure and servicing the accommodation in accordance with the terms of the lease, with no separate service charge as such being paid to the landlord.

Service charges will, in the main, be encountered in multi-tenanted buildings where occupiers share certain areas in common with other tenants. In these circumstances, the building will usually be administered by, or on behalf of, the landlord in for example, cleaning and lighting of the common parts, maintenance of lifts and other plant serving the whole building, and repairs and maintenance of the structural fabric with the costs incurred being recovered in due proportion from each tenant.

The means of calculating an individual tenant's service charge will depend on the provisions contained in the lease but typically for office buildings, a percentage will be derived from the floor area of the leased premises as a proportion of the net lettable area of the building as a whole. The lease document will sometimes express the percentage figure but often will simply provide for service charges to be recovered in a fair proportion. Wording differs from lease to lease and so it is essential for tenants to be aware of the provisions relating to their own occupation and to understand the calculation upon which the charges are demanded.

Throughout the term of a lease, a tenant may find little opportunity to negotiate the amount of service charge to be paid but should make sure they are satisfied that all sums demanded are reasonable by having regard to the lease provisions. When entering an FRI lease, the tenant should seek to ensure that, as in all aspects of the lease, the service charge provisions accurately reflect what is intended.

VAT

The changes brought about by the Finance Act 1989 have now been with us for some years and are well documented by property and accounting professions. In broad terms, much of the effect of the legislation was to change the VAT status of commercial property transactions involving supplies of land, civil engineering and construction services. The impact this has had on occupiers depends greatly on their own VAT status and thus the proportion of their input tax they are able to recover. There are, therefore, significant implications for those businesses making VAT exempt or partially exempt supplies who are unable or only partly able to recover VAT incurred.

By way of illustration, such occupiers may incur a VAT burden on their leasehold premises where a landlord opts, under the legislation, to waive exemption in respect of the building and so charge VAT on rent and other supplies made in connection with the property. VAT implications may also arise for tenants on other leasehold transactions such as surrenders and assignments involving capital sums or premiums.

VAT considerations will also apply to those purchasing a freehold interest or on the development of a building for their own occupation.

The full provisions of the legislations are far reaching and only a sample illustration of where an occupier might encounter an increased VAT burden has been given here. It is an area for specialist advice which should be sought if the position is unclear when considering specific projects or transactions.

JCT Contracts

The term JCT Contract is often euphemistically used to describe the contract entered into by both a client and contractor for the construction of a building. To the uninitiated this may appear to be fairly straightforward, however the euphemism belies the complexity and importance attached to entering into a contract with a builder.

JCT is an acronym for Joint Contract Tribunal, which comprises representatives of:

- Royal Institute of British Architects
- National Federation of Building Trade Employers
- Royal Institution of Chartered Surveyors
- Scottish Building Contract Committee
- Association of County Councils
- Association of Metropolitan Authorities
- Greater London Councils
- Association of District Councils
- Committee of Association of Specialist Engineering Contracts
- Federation of Associations of Specialists and Sub-contractors
- Association of Consultancy Engineers
- Confederation of British Industry.

The basic function of the JCT is to produce standard forms for building contracts which both the client and the builder can at relative ease enter into. The forms deal not only with the simplistic matters of 'the builder undertakes to carry out the works, and the client to pay for it', but also such weightier matters as variations to the contract, payment provisions, liabilities and what to do in the event of a dispute.

There is an array of JCT standard forms of building contracts, which are constantly updated to reflect the decisions of current precedents in law, as well as modern practices. As such it is always advisable to seek the

251

guidance of an industry professional, as to which standard form to use, and what obligations the contract imposes both on the client and his professional advisers ie Architects, Engineers, Quantity surveyors, and on the builder.

Whilst one of the key functions of JCT is to minimise the risk taken by the client and builder when entering into a contract, the innovative nature of construction will always provide an element of the unknown.

Building regulations

The purpose of Building Regulations is to ensure that in all new buildings public Health and Safety is maintained. Building Regulations have been in existence for some 100 years, and were originally introduced to prevent the haphazard sub-standard buildings that arose during the Industrial Revolution.

Building regulations are enforced through the auspices of the Local Authorities, and through Section 61 of the Public Health Act of 1936. The purpose is to ensure the structural stability, fire protection, damp prevention, drainage, sanitation and ventilation aspects of all buildings are maintained at current modern standards.

Checklist

- Property ownership
  - Do not forget that ownership can also be interpreted as long leases of say 99 years or more.

- Leasing
  - A lease is simply a contract between landlord and tenant, and although it can look complicated on paper most of the mysteries can be broken down by asking simple questions.

- Statutory controls
  - Planning permissions, building regulations, fire certificates and health and safety legislation.

- Uniform business rate
  - A rateable value based on levels of rent as at 1 April 1988 with a 'multiplier' factor set nationally.

- Service charges
  - A charge levied by the landlord, usually in multi-tenanted buildings, for common services, eg cleaning, lighting, maintenance.

- VAT
  - VAT on commercial property is a complicated issue, and specialist advice should be sought when considering specific projects or transactions.

- JCT contracts
  - 'Standard' contracts used in the construction industry.

- Building regulations
  - These help to prevent sub standard building practices.

About the Authors

John Grigg is Marketing Manager of First Move Facilities Management (FM²), which is a wholly owned subsidiary of the Allied Dunbar and BAT Group of companies. He has an extensive background in management consultancy and operational line management in large organisations in the private and public sectors. He has worked with smaller companies, both in the UK and overseas, and spent some years based in the Middle East introducing modern management techniques to local companies. He moved into premises and facilities management in the early 1980's when running a large service department within Allied Dunbar. He is a regular contributor to journals and seminars on general and facilities management topics.

Alan Jordan is head of Business Development at First Move Facilities Management (FM²). He is a Chartered Engineer, a member of the Institute of Mechanical Engineers and had a career in operational and project engineering management spanning 15 years before becoming a facilities manager in the mid 1980's. Since then he has been involved in most aspects of premises management, property strategy and building construction programmes. He recently completed an office accommodation study and proposed a strategy which has enabled Allied Dunbar to vacate three buildings with significant cost benefits. He is also a member of the Environmental Policy Group dealing with 'green' property issues. He is a regular presenter on facilities management seminars.

Contributors. Other contributors from FM² have enabled this book to be produced and the authors would like to acknowledge the significant input from:

David Buckley	–	Premises Manager
Ian Gamble	–	Facilities Manager
David Gibney	–	Building Services Manager
Fred Guscott	–	Assistant Director, Premises & Services
Richard Handley	–	Network Services Operations Manager (Allied Dunbar)
Martyn Hayward	–	Premises Manager
Malcolm Jones	–	Group Purchasing and Distribution Manager
Steven Marshall	–	Engineering & Technical Services Manager
David Miller	–	Executive Director, Premises & Services
Tim Miller	–	Environment Policy Advisor (Allied Dunbar)
Terry Mills	–	Project Design Engineer
Arthur Mitchell	–	Communications Manager
Robin Phelps	–	Health & Safety Advisor
Adrian Rushby	–	Premises Manager

Acknowledgement

This book could never have been produced without a number of key players, all of whom made a significant contribution to both the book and the enjoyment of its production. In particular thanks are extended to Jaclyn Stanley, Stewart Chapman, David Vessey and Fran McCaskill.